REAL ESTATE

Stories of passion, resilience and breaking barriers in the real estate industry

MAGGIE ANTILLON-MATHEWS

LATINAS IN REAL ESTATE

© Copyright 2022, Latinas in Real Estate
All rights reserved.

All rights reserved. No portion of this book may be reproduced by mechanical, photographic or electronic process, nor may it be stored in a retrieval system, transmitted in any form or otherwise be copied for public use or private use without written permission of the copyright owner.

This book is a compilation of stories from numerous people who have each contributed a chapter and is designed to provide inspiration to our readers.

It is sold with the understanding that the publisher and the individual authors are not engaged in the rendering of psychological, legal, accounting or other professional advice. The content and views in each chapter are the sole expression and opinion of its author and not necessarily the views of Fig Factor Media, LLC.

For more information visit:

Fig Factor Media, LLC | www.figfactormedia.com

Cover Design and layout by LDG Juan Manuel Serna Rosales
Printed in the United States of America

ISBN: 978-1-957058-15-3
Library of Congress Number: 2022906084

I dedicate this book to all of the women in the world. We all have our stories and gifts to share with others. We are all authors of our own BESTSELLING BOOK!

TABLE OF CONTENTS

Acknowledgments 6

Preface by Marki Lemons-Ryhal 8

AUTOR CHAPTERS

1. MAGGIE ANTILLON-MATHEWS

    Living Out My Motto 15

2. MICHELLE APONTE BOKSA

    We Can Have it All 25

3. AINHOA GARCIA

    Sprouting a Career in Real Estate 35

4. DANICA MATOS

    My Latina Real Estate Experience 45

5. MARISOL FRANCO

    Mi Destino (My Destiny) 55

6. TANYA DIAZ

    Overcome with Gratitude 65

7. TINA MARIE HERNANDEZ

    Figuring it Out 75

8. SHEYLA PADILLA
A Leap of Faith 85

9. BAXTIE RODRIGUEZ
The Falling Dream 97

10. ROSY BELTRAN
Real Estate with Heart 107

11. JOHANNA DIAZ
Following My Entrepreneurial Soul 117

12. MAGALY "MAGGIE" MARTINEZ
A Place to Call Home 127

13. CARMEN CHUCRALA
From Fallen Empire to Family Legacy 137

14. SALLY DELGADO
El Pan De Vida (The Bread of Life) 147

15. GINA DIAZ
My American Dream 157

About The Author 167

ACKNOWLDEGMENTS

First and foremost, I would like to thank GOD for his never-ending grace, love, and strength that He has given to me throughout my life, and the opportunities that have come before me. I never dreamed I would have an opportunity to write this or any other book. But like many things in my life, God has led me to places of growth, discovery, and purpose by connecting me with special people who have believed in me and helped to solidify who I want to be in this world.

One of those has been Jackie Camacho and the Today's Inspired Latina community. Thank you for believing in my humble story, and for giving me and many others the platform to make our voices resonate with others and inspire great things.

By creating this book, I aspire to inspire others. And I am grateful to those who have supported me in this mission.

To my book sisters, colleagues, and all the women along the way who have helped me persevere and believe all things possible; many of them appear in this book. They give me the courage to continue moving forward.

To the people who have taken part in putting these stories together: the editors, our author concierge, and everyone else it takes to make this magic happen.

Last and most importantly, I thank my incredible family and friends. Thank you to my mom and dad, who always believed in me and supported me through my failures and successes (and kept lending me money to survive).

To my husband, Tony Mathews, who has been incredibly supportive and very patient these last few years while I grew my business and pursued my goals. And to my beautiful daughter, Sofia, who is now ten years old, who is my daily inspiration to be the best I can be. I want to show her that with God by her side she can accomplish all of her wildest dreams.

Lastly, I want to give a very special and sincere thank you to my dearest sister, Christina Granados. No one else truly knows what I have experienced in the last fifteen years of my career; she has been with me through it all. Although on many occasions she wanted to do it, she has never left my side. We are complete opposites, but she is my biggest cheerleader and protector. I don't know where I would be without her and can truly say that she has made these last ten years of working here the most fun I've ever had. I am forever grateful for this magical opportunity and encourage everyone to put their story on paper.

PREFACE

Latinos not only comprise more than half of the nation's population growth over the past ten years, but they are also a growing force in the real estate profession. Maggie Antillon recognized that they have a wonderful story to tell about the industry and their place in it. That's how *Latinas in Real Estate* was born.

Maggie and I first connected through social media. Over the years, we've had the opportunity to break bread and exchange ideas about the real estate market and how to best serve our respective target audiences. She was focused on the Latino market and I on the African-Americans, but we shared a dedication to helping first-time homebuyers have a good experience.

Today, I'm a global real estate keynote speaker, a best-selling author, and a podcaster who addresses Latinos in the market. I've noted their rise in the world of real estate and have seen the valuable assets they bring to each interaction. With a strong sense of family values and critical bilingual skills, they place the American Dream into the hands of hardworking families who strive for financial security. Often they even do it after taking their real estate license exam in their second language! That's dedication!

One of the things I help Realtors with most is creating systems for them to grow their businesses through relationship. Because Latinas inherently understand the value of relationship, I know they spend a LOT of time having conversations and learning about others. I also know it's not easy to keep track of all that information. It requires automation. As a MBA and real estate educator, I tell Realtors that the best way to use customer details to turn an acquaintanceship into a relationship is with a customer relationship management (CRM) system. It's a main recommendation I make to real estate professionals who come to my distance learning classes to improve their return on investment (ROI). But it does more than help you increase revenue; it can make you unforgettable!

THE POWER OF CUSTOMER RELATIONSHIPS

The ladies in this book understand that nurturing customer relationships can lead to valuable, measurable results. Today, I operate my business at a 3 percent cost of goods sold and a 59.4 percent profitability by implementing strategies to improve customer relationships. I couldn't have done it without growing relationships and referrals, and that required a CRM.

CRMs keep track of all the important information we Realtors need to know to stay in relationship with current and potential clients. I teach the importance of identifying family, occupation, recreation, and dreams (FORD). for each contact in a Realtor's CRM system. Every day people share their FORD with the world via social media, email, and text messaging. FORD can help you understand your clients' pain points and desires, and should be inputted into CRM daily.

I also like to spend at least one hour every work day going through Facebook and LinkedIn and identifying each person's birthday, promotions, accomplishments, and favorite activities. I challenge real estate professionals to implement an "8 x 8" campaign where you make eight people feel special by 8 a.m. daily via email, messaging, or mailing them something of value. You also can do it with your own social media by sharing your own personal values, systems, and intentions too so your contacts who follow you can share, like, comment, and get to know your FORD, too.

In our business, it's so easy to get bogged down by distractions, inefficiency, and a lack of boundaries. But when we're not getting the results we want, our daily work routine is the first area we need to examine. For example, we need to know our numbers. To earn $100,000 per year, you need to add 2,880 contacts to your CRM system if your average price point is $250,000. These actions statistically will net you twenty closed real estate transactions. To accomplish your six-figure earning goals, you need to add eight new contacts to your CRM or connect in a meaningful way to the contacts who are already in your system. Separate the essentials from what's not moving the business forward to become effective and unstoppable. Every time you generate a new lead, communicate in a meaningful way, or initiate a one-on-one with a contact, add, or update the connection in your CRM.

Working this way also helps you to moderate your working hours. I believe you don't have to be open 24/7 to succeed in our profession. Don't buy into the lie that building a competitive real estate business requires you to give up all of your free time. If you work smarter, not harder, it's possible to have a thriving business without eighty-hour weeks and burnout. Work by relationship and referral. Agents who grow by nurturing their database dictate their schedule, work manageable hours, and are better equipped for market shifts.

REALTORS ARE ENTREPRENEURS

Many people don't realize that when they jump into real estate, they are becoming an entrepreneur, which means they have to operate like an entrepreneur. Simply having a real estate license doesn't make you an entrepreneur. You must build the entrepreneurial skills to grow your business.

For example, I was raised in the restaurant industry. When I launched a barbeque and meat rub into the marketplace, I had a master of business administration (MBA) but had not acquired all the skills necessary for entrepreneurship. So, I entered a self-employment project. It sharpened my skills in the areas that every entrepreneur needs, like leadership, management, marketing, and business development. I could never have been successful had I not taken that step.

It's often the same with new Realtors. Many lack the skills they need to build their business. They don't have a sales background and may never have been an entrepreneur. Luckily, nowadays, it's easier to find education in entrepreneurship at the community college, or through business associations or accelerator programs. I highly recommend these to any Realtor, who wants to launch or grow their real estate business.

Another challenge arises when others around us don't see us as a real estate entrepreneur. This is because, today, Realtors often have one or two other jobs. True, real estate can be a lucrative side hustle or fallback profession. For those of us doing real estate full time as a dedicated professional, however, it's important that those around us, especially in our inner social circle, understand we mean business. If there are people in your social circle, who are not doing business with you, find out why. It's our responsibility to change our language, demeanor, and how we present ourselves both in-person and online so others see us as a bona fide, dedicated, real estate professional.

I speak from experience. It took time for me to become a trusted advisor in real estate. I had to talk about it, wrap my car, and advertise. I promoted myself and have been quoted in many national publications. It was my responsibility to show people the real estate professional I was, and it is your responsibility to show your own value as a real estate agent, too.

Social media is a powerful tool to teach people this lesson but things don't change with one Facebook post. It happens over time when people see you in the context of a real estate agent. It takes persistence, professionalism and strategy—the same qualities that the ladies in this book have shown to become the successes they are today.

As you read the stories in this book that trace the triumphs and the tragedies of life in this beloved industry, learn from the ways these ladies have moved their businesses forward through building relationships. I'm encouraged by what I've seen from Latinas in real estate and expect to see more of them in leadership positions, presidencies, and chairmanships. They are the willing volunteers, the visionaries, the connectors, and the ones putting the "E" in diversity, equity and inclusion (DEI) by helping first-time homebuyers find their way, unencumbered, to the American dream. Their future is bright and I'm excited to watch them lead the way!

Marki Lemons-Ryhal
Global real estate keynote speaker
Realtor, Best-selling author
Podcaster
www.markilemons.com
#Lipedema

LIVING OUT MY MOTTO

MAGGIE ANTILLON-MATHEWS

"My greatest accomplishment has been NEVER giving up."

A few weeks ago, I came across a picture of my very first headshot as a Realtor. I vividly remember my twenty-six-year-old self in a blue blouse, starting a new career and wondering where the journey would lead. You see, I was not born a natural entrepreneur. Quite the opposite. I always felt born to serve and that I, single-handedly, could change the world. I definitely got that trait from my father, who always demonstrated empathy and spoke through his continuous efforts of giving back and assisting others.

Every day I try to live out my personal motto:

Serve someone every day.

Add value to people every day.

Put people first every day.

SERVE SOMEONE EVERY DAY

As the eldest of four children, I was born and raised in Chicago by parents who were the first of their families to immigrate to the United States. I inherited the great responsibility of having to figure things out on my own, without the benefit of relatives already in the United States. My parents worked in factory jobs all of their lives and were the most hardworking people I've ever known. They worked opposite schedules to make sure that one of them was always at home with me and my siblings. My dad sacrificed to make sure we grew up in a safe neighborhood, even when that meant taking extra shifts and spending less time with the family.

One day I was watching *Oprah* on TV and saw a counselor who worked with teenagers. She seemed to really make a difference in their lives so, I was convinced that is what I wanted to do. After graduation, I pursued a degree in behavioral science and when I was finished, I went to work for the Illinois Department of Children and Family and Services (DCFS) as a case manager. I connected well with the teens, but there was only so much influence you could have on them, given the bureaucracy of the system.

I had a friend who was going to a real estate class, and it sounded interesting to me because I always liked interior design and the transformation of spaces. I took the class and passed the test. My approach was so service-minded that when I joined my first brokerage in 2001, I didn't really understand that I was entering a career in sales. The brokerage was down the street from my home, so I thought that was a good enough reason to work there. I also thought that clients would be assigned to me and I would have lots of walk-ins. Boy was I wrong!

I took on the daughter of one of my mom's friends as my first client. I was amazed when I saw that the commission from my first sale replaced two months of income! I then realized if I brought my heart and my attitude of servitude into my work, no matter what I was doing, I could help people and make an impact on their lives. DCFS wasn't the only way. I could do it as a real estate agent, too!

I felt very alone at the beginning of my career. I can still remember my white-haired managing broker sitting in his office saying, "Let me know if you need anything." I had no idea what I needed! My first five years in real estate were very slow, but I had a safety net because I was living at home. When I turned 30, I bought my first property. Meanwhile, I built my business by approaching people to educate, rather than sell. My goal was relationship-building, and that's what eventually got me where I am. I built a referral network through my relationships.

In 2005, at the peak of the real estate market, I was still inexperienced, but I had closed a couple of deals, which kept me interested in real estate. However, in 2008 when the housing market crashed, so did I.

I was a broker. I was broken, and I was broke!

To paraphrase Napoleon Hill, every failure can be a blessing in disguise to teach you something valuable. I did not know it at the time, but the market crash would become a tremendous blessing in my life.

BRING VALUE EVERY DAY

I had to make a decision: go back to doing social work or keep pursuing my goals in real estate. I remember someone saying to me, "Maggie, if you want to do better, you have to know better!" So, I began a journey of knowledge and self-empowerment.

Through networking and connecting with the right people, I was introduced to books like *Think and Grow Rich*, and *Rich Dad, Poor Dad*. My world expanded! Listening to the teachings of Zig Ziglar and Jim Rohn truly helped me shift my mindset and understand that I could succeed in real estate. I had the power to accomplish whatever I set out to do, and my only limits were self-imposed.

I began to change my internal conversations. I became more self-aware and decided that I wouldn't say anything to myself that I wouldn't say to someone else. I understood the power of words. I was my own worst critic and that was hindering me from moving forward. With a new perspective on myself and armed with everything I had learned, I forged ahead in real estate . . . and became successful!

Today, I lead one of the industry's fastest growing brokerage firms. We are ranked #22 of 4,000 offices. We are breaking ground and creating unimaginable opportunities. My work has filled me with purpose and the desire to impact others on a higher level. However, every day I try to bring value and share my knowledge and experience with those who can benefit from it.

In my younger days, I never really had a mentor; I learned through trial and error. That's why it's so important for me to serve as a mentor, pay forward my experience, and offer people opportunities. We all have it within us to succeed but we also need someone to believe in us. Mentoring is my way of bringing value to the lives of others. It's amazing to witness the magic of those you've helped succeeding so wonderfully! I also continue to sow seeds that will grow later. I'm truly thankful for even the smallest way I can help someone become more successful in their real estate career.

PUT PEOPLE FIRST EVERY DAY

Zig Ziglar once wrote, "You will get all you want in life if you help enough other people get what they want." This idea came alive for me in a real way recently when I attended a John Maxwell leadership conference. Now, I see things in a different light—a light that has illuminated yet another road for me.

I am inspired every single day by the efforts of people just trying to better themselves—people with different stories, from different walks of life, just trying to take care of their families, and build something sustainable for their future and generations. I get to be a small part of that process as the universe continues to connect me with amazing people. Although I'm no John Maxwell, I know that my superpower is to help people, and through my work as an educator and servant leader, I can inspire others to follow their goals and dreams.

I also know who I want to be, and that I want to be a transformational leader of myself and others. I want to add value to people's lives so they, in turn, will add value to the lives of others. It's a ripple effect.

Since collaborating on my second anthology, *Today's Inspired Latina Volume IX*, I can see my life transforming right before my eyes. I have met the most amazing women, mentors, and friends who have taken me to a place I did not know even existed. The friendships that I have made, the connections that I have built, and the people that I have surrounded myself with have given me a new perspective on what I can accomplish on my journey to self-happiness. I also have seen many women transform, bloom, and unleash all of their potential. Just as they have inspired me, I hope I have inspired them. It's been a beautiful thing to witness this reciprocal support and to help each other grow.

I know from my experiences navigating the waters of my career that no one is responsible for the pursuit of my success except me. I will always be responsible for asking for what I want. I believe closed mouths don't get fed. You have to raise your hand, and ask to be part of the conversation.

THE REWARD

In early 2021, I received a message from my sister, Christina, that she had found a nomination letter from the Chicago Association of Realtors® in my spam folder. I was incredibly surprised to hear I was a possible candidate for the prestigious Managing Broker of the Year award! To be honored by someone outside of my organization meant the world to me, but the due date for entry was that day. I knew that I had missed an incredible opportunity, but as they say at the Oscars, "It was an honor just to be nominated." Never in my wildest dreams would I guess that someone from the Chicago Association of REALTORS® would personally reach out to me the following Monday and encourage me to apply, even though the deadline had passed. I got to work and quickly turned in my application with an enormous feeling of gratitude.

A few weeks later, I received the email that would change my life.

I vividly recall walking down the red carpet in my red dress, and onto the stage at the Hilton Hotel on Michigan Avenue in downtown Chicago to accept my award for the 2021 Managing Broker of the Year. My dad gave me a standing ovation and received me back at the table with open arms and tear-filled eyes. That evening I felt proud to not only make a positive impact on my community and my peers but also proud to be the daughter of an immigrant from Chihuahua, Mexico, who fought for many years to stay in this country and provide a better opportunity for his children. I am his American dream.

Countless failures have led me to where I am today. I often took risks because I knew that there was always a lesson in failure and an opportunity to move forward. I describe my career as a series of failures that have led to accomplishments or valuable knowledge, all because I was placed in those difficult situations.

Self-doubt, fear of not being good enough, and fear of people finding out who I "really was"—the dreaded "imposter syndrome"—have made me question whether I would ever succeed. Today, I can truly say that I am proud of what I have accomplished and the work that I have put in, but my greatest accomplishment is NEVER giving up.

Once again, I enter a new and different phase in my life. Now I can say no to anything not in line with my personal motto, that does not make me happy, or is not fulfilling. I can say no to anything unhelpful, that steers me away from my full potential. It is a phase where I am trying to establish healthy boundaries, and I am a work in process. I have made sacrifices, and will continue to do so, but not at the price of the most important things in my life.

The twenty-year career mark has made me reflect on many things in my life, and I am ready to embark on yet another journey where I can take two decades of knowledge, experience, failures, and successes and share them with the world. I am entering a new chapter in my life with a new understanding of the power within me. The more I learn with each passing day, the more I realize that I have so much more to learn, and I know it. The quest for knowledge and self-improvement is never-ending!

MY REAL ESTATE INSPIRATION

My career has challenged me in more ways than I could ever imagine, but those challenges have prepared me for the present and the future. Some people make it look easy. But with success, there is a price to pay. You will have to put in the hard work and the long hours, and it requires endurance. You will need patience and the understanding that things do not, and will not, happen overnight. Faith in God, or a higher power is important to keep you grounded and faithful, but most importantly, you will have to understand what matters most to you. This is something that I wish I had learned earlier in my career.

As women, especially Latina women who have seen their parents work hard and sacrifice, we have this idea that we have to do the same in order to get to the top. I have certainly paid the price and sacrificed my well-being and time with my family before realizing that something had to change. When I stopped to reevaluate what was most important to me, I found that when the universe is constantly evolving, it is crucial to stop on occasion and look at where you are, and where you want to be, in order to evolve with it.

WE CAN HAVE IT ALL

MICHELLE APONTE BOKSA

"Confidence is key to breaking barriers and having it all as working Latinas."

I was sitting with a recruiter, sipping my freshly brewed coffee and admiring her beautiful floral skirt and five-inch stiletto heels. She was upbeat and very personable; however, I was not sure if I should have said yes to this meeting.

My mind was wandering . . . how does she walk so easily in those shoes? How am I supposed to attend this women's event she is hosting if I don't have a babysitter for my toddler? Then she made a comment that caught me off-guard. "I've been talking with my friends about whether we (women) can have it all." I cannot recall what else she said, but I certainly did not understand why this was up for debate. I firmly commented that yes, we can. We can have a career, still be mothers and wives, and live a balanced life.

Today, I am proving it.

In hindsight, I never expected to have a career in real estate. Like many people, I did not know what I wanted to do with my life, and I also did not understand what options were available. All I knew was that my parents expected me to graduate from college, and I was the first one in my family to do so. College turned out to be a stepping-stone for my personal and professional development. Thereafter, the decision to work as a residential mortgage loan originator was easy; however, the journey has been quite a challenge. Now, my career in real estate creates a comfortable lifestyle for me and my family and it can do the same for you.

YEARS IN TRAINING

My family is from Puerto Rico, and both my parents were born in neighboring towns on the island. My father is one of six siblings and rose from humble beginnings to become a business owner. He grew up in a two-room house without a television or running water and dropped out of elementary school at a young age to work on the sugar cane plantation with my grandfather. He moved to Chicago in his late teens and has been self-employed for over thirty years. My dad has strong people skills, is hard-working and a risk-taker. These attributes helped him support our large family.

My mom shares similar traits and also has been a provider

for our family. She moved to Chicago at a young age and completed a year of college before becoming a mother. My mom raised four kids, supported my dad with his different businesses, took care of extended family, built a successful career in real estate as a mortgage loan originator, and even eventually returned to school to earn her bachelor's degree. She set the bar high for her children, and she is my idol, my best friend and presently, my business partner.

As a child, I was cooking, cleaning, and changing diapers when I was only ten years old. My childhood was a bit sheltered because I spent very little time outside of the house other than school. My family had one car, and since my parents did not allow anyone else to drive me to or from events, I did not have a chance to join any sports or extracurricular activities. Learning to complete household chores and look after my younger siblings taught me a great deal of responsibility and discipline early in life. However, the lack of social interaction outside of school made me shy, well into my adult years.

When I was a teenager, our family's lifestyle changed due to my mom's booming career in the real estate industry. The rise of household income allowed us to buy a second car, a larger house, and enjoy regular family vacations. I was even lucky enough to have a quinceañera celebration and my very own car by age sixteen. It was then that I made the decision to strive for financial security and be able to share the same experiences with my future family. I was determined to have it all.

FROM WALKING TO RUNNING

In 2003, I took my first job in the mortgage industry as a receptionist for my mom's mortgage brokerage. I worked weekdays and attended college in the evenings. Within the first year, I was processing loans, and after completing my bachelor's degree in 2006, I became a licensed mortgage loan originator. However, I did not have the confidence to pursue this career, and I struggled with my performance.

I was a timid twenty-two-year-old; asking for leads was completely out of my comfort zone. I was afraid to make cold calls, did not want to feel rejected, and was concerned about pay as it was a commission-only position. Looking back, I realize that I was full of excuses. In lieu of going through training and working on personal and professional development, I picked up a part-time job and spent far less time pursuing the career. Over the next three years, the housing bubble burst, the economy went into recession, and the brokerage closed.

In 2009, I decided to return to school. I began an MBA program, as I thought this would open a different opportunity in the financial services sector. At work, I supported three top producers and was closing 300 loan applications per year as a sales assistant. Not only was I closing a high volume of loan applications but I was also mastering underwriting guidelines and creating workflows to make the loan process run as smoothly as possible for all parties. I designed a great tracking tool and established strong relationships with the loan processing team.

When I graduated from the master of business

administration (MBA) program in 2012, I had built enough self-confidence to pursue a career as a mortgage loan originator. I saved enough money to cover six months of living expenses and did all the sales activities I avoided seven years earlier.

My network was small, and I did not have any referral partners, so I had to start off with whatever tools were available to me. The company I worked for did not offer any sort of mentorship or training program, but they did offer Zillow leads. I worked with these internet leads and created social media accounts to connect with family, friends, and old classmates. I also started cold-calling prospective referral partners. Since I did not have prior sales experience, I asked my mom for tips and learned by trial and error. I remained motivated, consistent, and committed. In 2014, my first calendar year in business, I had earned the same income as I did in my previous role as a sales assistant.

THE BALANCING ACT

When I started my career as a mortgage loan originator, I didn't realize that being in this sales role meant that I would essentially be running my own business. Initially, I was working by myself, managing the whole process from marketing to closing. My business came in waves because I was not able to work on the business while I was in the business. I also experienced many life events in the first several years that impacted business development—loss, family illness, marriage, and the birth of my sweet baby boy, Yuri.

Becoming a mother challenged me in ways I never imagined. Meeting the demands of a new baby, dealing with sleep deprivation for eighteen months, and growing a business was difficult, to say the least. I would no longer be available to complete preapproval letters at ten o'clock on a Friday night or to answer every phone call. Long-term relationships quickly waned because of the boundaries I created for my new lifestyle.

I was overwhelmed with the situation because I lacked processes for managing a growing business. I was continually working fifty hours a week with only part-time childcare and was constantly playing catch up, both at work and at home. My husband and I shared some household responsibilities, and whenever he offered to do more, I quickly declined as I felt it was my responsibility as the woman of the house.

The hardest year for me was 2020, and not just because of the pandemic. With a two-year-old at home, I regrettably bought into the culture of overwork and was working twice as hard as I ever did. My days started painfully early at four o'clock in the morning, jam-packed with mommy duties between work calls, texts, emails, and endless cups of coffee that carried me through to midnight. With a two-person team, I managed to double business from the year before. We closed over 200 loans totaling more than $52 million in volume, which is a typical yield for a three to four-person team. I seemed to be "having it all," but instead, I was headed for trouble as I had sacrificed my boundaries and my self-care.

After months of facing relentless chest pains and nausea,

I experienced a severe anxiety attack that left me in a nervous state of mind for quite some time. The thought of having another anxiety attack was debilitating, and I had to make immediate lifestyle changes in order to survive. I finally accepted the help offered by my husband, family, and friends. I also implemented the following tips to my routine: limiting my work hours, reducing excessive caffeine intake, journaling, and practicing meditation. My sister became my accountability meditation partner and we practiced yoga every single morning for six straight months. I knew that if we were connecting by video chat at seven o'clock in the morning, I was going to be OK that day. I am so grateful to have tremendous support from my tribe as they all played a vital role in my road to recovery.

To improve time management in the workplace without compromising productivity, I restructured the business and established a framework for a larger team. Then I pursued a new role as a branch manager to allow me the option to hire additional team members as needed. This model was built with a vision for growth and flexibility. I now can take time off in the middle of the week for a personal errand, a trip to the museum with my son, or a visit with my abuela (grandmother) to give her a manicure and the business will continue to run on its own. This has improved my quality of life and enhanced the efficiency in my business. I have built a foundation where other loan originators can grow a successful business in real estate and balance family life, too.

SERVING THE COMMUNITY

Being a Latina has given me an opportunity to bridge the gap of homeownership among the minority communities. I offer various online and in-person educational homebuyer events and use my bilingual skills to bring financial literacy to all those in need. Also, since I specialize in assisting first-time buyers, who typically do not have a trusted financial advisor, I fill this role by educating them about their largest investment—their home. If they need additional financial assistance or legal guidance, I will refer them to other trusted professionals.

When the pandemic hit, I felt an even greater need to give back to the community. I organized fundraisers to provide holiday meals for seniors and for the Greater Chicago Food Depository, as well as several other nonprofit organizations that help provide basic needs for those in the Chicagoland area.

As I reflect on the community service projects created thus far, I realize how much my network has grown. This journey has been rewarding and has provided opportunities that I never would have thought possible. It all began with self-confidence and the willingness to try. Confidence is key to breaking barriers and having it all as working Latinas.

MY REAL ESTATE INSPIRATION

My career in real estate was inspired by the financial security it offered my family, but it has provided so much more. I have learned how to communicate effectively with others, run a business, and invest in real estate. Moreover, I have learned the need for personal growth to succeed in life. To pursue a career in real estate, I urge you to learn from the professionals, network, and find a mentor. Each individual will offer a different definition of success, and learning from a variety of sources will provide wide-ranging experience, knowledge, and inspiration.

In addition, ask yourself these questions:

- What is my biggest inspiration for working in the real estate industry?
- How does my inspiration align with my personal and professional goals?
- How would my life be impacted if I had the ability to create my own work schedule and/or business model with uncapped income?

Here are a few book recommendations to help with personal growth and sales tips:

- *How to Win Friends and Influence People by Dale Carnegie*
- *The Miracle Morning* by Hal Elrod
- *Never Split the Difference: Negotiating as if Your Life Depended on it* by Chris Voss and Tahl Raz

Should you have any additional questions, I am happy to be a resource.

BIOGRAPHY

Michelle Aponte Boksa specializes in assisting first-time homebuyers and excels at breaking the homebuying process into simple steps. Her mission is to educate clients on loan options so they can make informed decisions and plan for the future. She provides clear, upfront information about the mortgage process so her clients feel confident in their homebuying journey.

Michelle started working in real estate at the age of eighteen as a receptionist for a mortgage broker. After completing her MBA in 2012, she committed to becoming a top mortgage loan originator. She has been awarded Top Originator by the prestigious Scotsman Guide, the National Association of Hispanic Real Estate Professionals® (NAHREP) and has received the Freddie Mac Home Possible Rise Award along with various accolades from employers. Her long-term goal is to share her experience and provide a place for other loan originators to thrive in the industry.

Michelle's definition of success is to create things that bring value to others. She has created local fundraisers to provide basic needs for the less fortunate and welcomes new opportunities to serve the community. She also enjoys exploring the city with her four-year-old son, cooking with her husband, visiting family often, staying active, and learning new things.

Michelle Aponte Boksa
michelle@teamaponte.com
www.linkedin.com/in/michelleaponteboksa

SPROUTING A CAREER IN REAL ESTATE

AINHOA GARCIA

"All my childhood lessons gave me the necessary tools to navigate a world of entrepreneurship."

I have always wanted to live a life on my own terms, but I was never clear on how it would happen.

My roots were nurtured in the small village of Adamuz in Spain, where I enjoyed long afternoon walks, stories of civil war, and lots of house projects with Grandpa Francisco and Grandma Maria. She cooked in the *candela* (fireplace) every day, added a bit of bleach in the *'barreño'* (bucket) to make the dishes look cleaner, skillfully repurposed leftovers, and cared for me when I felt sick. She was beautiful, elegant, and a social butterfly.

My grandpa was a lucky man. He was the provider, the hunter, and the fighter. When I was two years old, he had a stroke and never fully recovered his ability to speak. Despite the difficulties, our communication was great. His blue eyes would get watery, his saliva would touch the outside of his lips and he would use his hands to help him communicate.

From my Grandma I learned genuine care, attention to details, and going the extra mile to exceed expectations. From my Grandpa I learned patience, empathy, and resilience. Nobody anticipated how important those traits would eventually become for me. I miss both of them dearly.

THE STEM

My mother would wake me up extra early so I could be the first one in line outside of preschool. My uniform was sharp, my hair was done, I smelled like baby powder, and my lunch was packed with love. Because I always arrived at school early and well-prepared for the day, I became the teachers' helper and the elected student representative every year. I loved doing homework, practicing theater and "belonging" in many places.

At home, I also wanted to do it all: cleaning, cooking and helping my mom manage the house. I just wanted to take some things off her plate. My family worked on someone else's

land, had farm animals, and hunted for living. During the olive picking season, my mom worked in the countryside. She would lose lots of weight and wouldn't get much sleep. My brother and I slept with our bedroom doors open while she cleaned the house at night. I can still smell the cleaning product she used to clean our home.

My father Francisco was a hard worker, but not the best

husband. He traveled often and spent free time away from home. He was involved in politics in the village and was respected and admired for instating many positive changes for Adamuz.

I have very few happy memories of my parents, my brother, and me as a family. It has taken me a long time to realize that parents make mistakes as adults and live through their own struggles and fears.

I am still discovering who Ana is as a woman.

THE FIRST LEAVES

I left home when I was 16. In my hometown, most students attended a community college about 15 minutes away by bus and returned home every night, but that was not for me. I wanted to study in the city of Cordoba. My parents were not happy with my decision, but I had already completed the paperwork and been admitted by the time I even told them.

I was the first person in my family to leave our hometown. In Cordoba, I met wonderful people, had my first love, and made life-changing decisions. I felt lucky to have a supportive family and live in a country of peace and opportunities. All I had to do was keep excellent grades so I would qualify for national grants that would allow me to finance my education. It was then I was presented with the opportunity to study abroad in France.

I packed my suitcase, said goodbye to my first love, and kissed my mom. During my first three months in Metz (La Lorraine, France), I lived with engineering students from Colombia and learned how to make *arepas*, dance *merengue,* and work as a team. After the Colombians left, I became closer to my Muslim neighbors, and I discovered a whole new world. From cooking with lots of spices and eating with our hands, to long conversations about the universe and the stars, our nights were endless. I keep these memories in a special corner of my heart.

When the International Student Program ended, I returned to Spain and finished the last year of University. One day in the cafeteria I saw an ad about becoming an *Au Pair* and living the American Dream. It seemed exciting, so I applied just to have an option after graduation. They called me the next day for an Interview in Madrid, and then a second one in Cordoba a couple weeks later. After I received my degree in Translation and Interpreting studies, it was time to pack again and move to the U.S.

THE BUD

I landed in Chicago by myself on September 24, 2012. My luggage decided to take a separate trip, but nothing was going to disturb my excitement for the new adventure. I lived with a non-traditional family and cared for a little sweet girl with special needs. On most days, I started work at five-thirty in the morning and ended at nine o'clock at night. Long hospital visits, daily breathing treatments, and syringes were part of an ordinary day in her life and mine. She taught me to face challenges with positivity.

I enjoyed exploring the vibrant city of Chicago during my time off. I remember the day I realized Chicago was going to be my home. I was sitting in the back seat of a ride share with three strangers, all from different ethnicities, driving down Lakeshore Drive. We spoke briefly, but it felt right. Looking at the impressive skyline I told myself, "I belong here."

I faced many challenges as an *au pair*, but I was encouraged by the adventure. I bought my first pair of pants at Express on North Avenue. The pants were seventy-eight dollars but the cashier told me I owed eighty-five dollars and eighty cents. That's when I learned about taxes and began to doubt if I would make it in America.

In Chicago, I made friends from all over the world. I have always believed life is like a train ride. Some people jump into our railcar and leave the train a few stations down the line. Others stay until the final destination. Those who depart early leave behind their memories, laughter, and lessons on the train. I am grateful for all of them.

THE PETALS

When the two-year *au pair* program ended, I decided to stay. I had created beautiful relationships and my dreams had grown immensely. I moved to a small studio apartment with bed bugs and loud neighbors. I also started a new job as a nanny for a kind Jewish family in Roscoe Village. They made me feel like part of their family and included me in their life celebrations. They even covered my plane ticket when I received one of the most painful calls of my life.

Almost four years after I had last hugged my grandma, she

was gone. I had been battling with Immigration to renew my status, I could not leave the country. I went to the immigration office on my knees and begged for empathy. I went back the next day too. A red-haired supervisor felt my pain and looked into my case. She found a special permit for me to return to Spain if I could show supporting documents of my bloodline to the deceased person. I was overjoyed and flew out that evening to say my last goodbye to my grandma.

THE BLOOMING

After recharging my battery in Spain, I returned to Chicago with the energy to conquer the world. Then, I told my boss I was going to look for a career job. She not only encouraged me to do so but helped revise my resume and find different places to apply. They mentioned real estate would be a great fit for me, but I had no clue what real estate was.

That evening, I plugged "real estate" into the search criteria on LinkedIn and applied for a position. They called me the next morning for an interview, and I had enough time to drop off the kids at school, go to Forever 21 to buy a blazer, and put some lipstick on. On my way to their office, I googled the job description and the best qualities of a candidate.

I soon learned I needed to take classes and pass an exam to work in real estate. I made a plan to make it happen. Once I had my license, I knew I had to be patient, coachable, and keep my other jobs to pay my bills.

Building a career in real estate is like being on a rollercoaster, but you don't know that when you start. The highs are really high, the lows hit hard, and your stomach can jump to your mouth in between. Nobody knew I was only a part-time agent because I worked around the clock, always took appointments, and consistently attended training and networking events. I left

the house at five-thirty in the morning and came home around eleven at night, every day. Every weekend. Every holiday.

Very early in my real estate journey, I decided I wanted to have a personal brand that made me known as a caring problem-solver and a knowledgeable resource for my clients. For the first six months of my career, I didn't own a car so I covertly arrived at all showings, open houses, and appointments via train, bus, or Uber. I became a pro at calculating arrival and commuting times to always arrive early. I would bring a pair of running shoes in my bag so I could run to catch my rides. The joy of having your first closing is hard to describe. For me, it was on a sunny Friday afternoon and my sunglasses hid my tears. I held the check and stared at the numbers for a while before depositing it.

On Saturday, I bought a brand-new car. I felt so happy. Now I had more time on my hands to help more clients. Putting people's best interests first had a snowball effect and my clientele started growing organically and consistently. The foundation of every sustainable sales business should be referral-based, and mine was, and still is today.

All my childhood lessons gave me the necessary tools to navigate a world of entrepreneurship. Some of my mentors told me, "Don't worry about money; serve people and the money will come." The next day was my last day as a part-time agent. I took a leap of faith, said goodbye to my amazing nanny family, and closed that chapter.

In July of 2019, I was first awarded as a Top Producer alongside other colleagues of Realty of Chicago. When I heard my name, I couldn't hold back my tears.

Twenty-Twenty was a year of tremendous business growth for me, despite the pandemic. Many other professional doors opened for me. I was introduced to NAHREP (National Association of Hispanic Real Estate Professionals®) and became the Event Director for the Chicago chapter in 2021. I started a team of my own and was recognized as the Platinum Top Producer at Realty of Chicago and was awarded by the Chicago Association of REALTORS®.

Then on March 8, 2021 my mom was diagnosed with cancer and the world stopped for me. My chest felt like I was being stabbed several times. I lost my breath, my vision got blurry and my heart got stuck in my throat. They say in times of adversity, you find out who your tribe is. My team stepped up, and even though I failed them many times, they kept the boat afloat.

So, I am here today in 2022, awaiting a year of understanding, acceptance, and recovery. My real estate journey will continue, and I know there will be more lessons to learn. I welcome them all.

MY REAL ESTATE INSPIRATION

Real estate is not just selling houses; it is entrepreneurship at its finest. Realtors wear many hats in each transaction: marketer, negotiator, financial advisor and even therapist, at times, all while managing a business as their own CFO, CEO, and lead generator. Every day is different in this career and I love that!

Real estate is a business of relationships, so you must love people. Make as many connections as you can. Opportunities flow as a result of those genuine interactions. Here are my top three tips for new real estate professionals:

- **Never stop learning.** Local, national and international associations and programs are available at your fingertips. New accreditations like buyer specialist, certified negotiator, digital marketing expert, etc. can add value to your skillset.
- **Find your niche.** Who is your target audience?
- **Be authentic everywhere you go.** That includes your presence on social media platforms.

BIOGRAPHY

Ainhoa Garcia graduated from the University of Cordoba in Spain and the University of Paul Verlaine in France in translation and interpreting studies. In 2012, Ainhoa packed her suitcase with a bunch of dreams and moved to Chicago. She has always had a passion for helping others, and saw a career in real estate as an opportunity to combine that passion with her love for interior design, business, and communication.

Having experienced the relocation process firsthand, she is committed to helping her clients make every transaction as memorable as possible, every step of the way. Ainhoa believes the best part of her job is the amazing people she meets and connects with. In 2019, she was introduced to Nahrep Chicago, and she currently serves as the elected Vice Presidentof the organization. In 2019, she was introduced to Nahrep Chicago, and she currently serves as the elected Vice President of the organization. First-time home buyers, people looking to sell, or folks just needing tips to update their home should have her number.

Driven by honesty, advocacy, and dedication, Ainhoa works with hundreds of loyal and wonderful clients and has created a growing team that has achieved top producer awards, both locally and nationally. When Ainhoa is not selling houses, you can find her "at brunch" in Chicago, traveling, or attending events. She also enjoys cooking, reading, volunteering, and preparing "to-do" lists.

Ainhoa Garcia
ainhoarealtor@gmail.com
Instagram: @ainhoarealtor

THE LATINA REAL ESTATE EXPERIENCE

DANICA MATOS

"My happiness is a daily choice."

It all started when I was twelve years old. I sat in the back seat of the car as my dad drove around, collecting cash from people in different places. Something clicked in my brain, and I became curious.

"Hey dad, why are these people giving you all this money?" I asked.

"Mamita, I own these properties and they have to pay me to live there," he responded.

SAY WHAT? I was immediately sold. My entrepreneurial spirit was born and more importantly, my love for all things real estate!

BEATING THE ODDS

I was raised in the Humboldt Park neighborhood of Chicago, where a large community of Puerto Ricans settled in the 1960s. Many of them owned real estate and small businesses like my father. However, growing up there from the late 1980s to the early 2000s, it became one of the most crime-ridden areas in the country and well known for drugs and gangs. I lived in this environment and even had family involved in that criminal lifestyle, but my parents created a completely different world for me.

My strict father taught me to be street smart, choose the right friends, be watchful and mindful of my surroundings, and to understand boys. I was raised to be very intellectual and fun-loving. My parents surrounded me with a ton of laughter and wonderful values. I never got involved in the illicit neighborhood activities.

Instead, I attended private school and played classical piano from age four through eighth grade! I had academic test scores so high that I was placed into Lane Tech College Prep High School, a top school in a much safer community. Since there were no college courses in real estate at that time, I attended DeVry University for computer programming and graduated with a four-year degree in just three years.

Soon, I was in corporate America, making more money at twenty-one years old than most of my family members. Then 9/11 hit. I lost my job, but this was my chance to do what I really wanted.

WORKING WITH INTEGRITY

After filing for unemployment, I immediately pursued my real estate license and earned it in 2003. I wanted to become an investor and build wealth. But first, I joined Betancourt Realty in Wicker Park, near my old neighborhood.

I was eager and ready to learn. The broker took me under his wing and taught me about networking, new construction, condo conversions, and how to gain business from developers. He helped me with open houses and taught me how to dress, what music to play, what food and drinks to bring, and how to talk to protentional buyers.

It was the "height of the market." We were all flying high and selling homes way over their true value. The lending industry had become very "creative," and many people were able to buy with no money down. I was working hard, learning fast, and making money! But I'll never forget my first deal.

I worked with a Mexican single mom who wanted to buy a home in the Little Village neighborhood, a very rough area at that time. At the closing, we found that the mortgage broker had lied his way to the closing table, so the deal fell apart. There I was, a new agent helping a single mom who was about to be homeless. I cried in the car all the way home. It was then I realized I needed to be a proactive problem-solver and a master at helping clients secure their deals. I learned everything I could, asked a million questions, and triple-checked everyone's work because I refused to allow such a thing to happen to one of my clients again.

In the mid-2000s, we had a lot of sharks and slicksters in

real estate. Even Latino professionals were taking advantage of other hardworking blue-collar Latinos who were deserving of their American dream to own a home. It was heartbreaking, and I refused to work alongside such professionals. After that first closing experience, I was careful to choose trustworthy mortgage brokers, attorneys, and inspectors. I created relationships with the best of the best.

I treat every person with the same integrity, regardless of the sale price of their home or the size of my commission check. This attitude and work ethic has sustained me in real estate. It's also the reason why other agents trust me and choose to work with me over others.

WEATHERING THE STORM

In 2006, I was twenty-seven years old and ready to become an investor. I bought my first investment multi-unit and my first single family home. I even invested $20,000 in a wealth-building institute to travel around the country and learn from the top investors and entrepreneurs. I started making offers and growing my portfolio in promising areas, like Las Vegas and Detroit. For a while it was amazing, and I was learning a lot and profiting. Those days will always have a special place in my heart. Then came the great housing market crash of our time!

My career in computers quickly started and ended with 9/11. Now my investor career was hit with another crisis. I lost everything and had to file bankruptcy, even though I had perfect credit and a relationship with a lender. My investment properties were worth pennies to the dollar. I couldn't sell them, and tenants lost their jobs and couldn't pay the rent.

It was a nightmare. I was only twenty-nine years old, and my two careers had burned up before my eyes. I was in debt for more than $1 million, and didn't even have money for groceries. I was ashamed to tell my family. Coincidentally, I volunteered at my church to run the food drive and was able to pack some grocery bags for myself!

God has always provided for my most important financial, spiritual, and emotional needs. Without my relationship with the Lord and my church community, I'm not sure how I would have overcome my massive debt and failure. It crushed my spirit for years. The hardest reality was to accept that my career as an investor was over.

REBUILDING WITH PURPOSE

Fortunately, I was able to find work in the real estate world in a salaried position because of my experience. I was no longer an entrepreneur, but I was able to pay the bills again. I joined a Christian church, served my community, and worked hard. I got back on my feet financially, but more importantly, spiritually and physiologically, too. I learned that not everything is about money. Your mental well-being, your community, family, faith, and enjoying the simple things in life that money cannot buy is much more important. Yes, wealth can improve your life and open doors to help give back to others, but it shouldn't be your greatest reason for living.

Those years were the hardest, but richest times. Misfortune can test you, but if you can find peace and joy when all you worked for is gone, you will become the best version of yourself. When the money returns, you'll appreciate it and make wiser choices. Since then, nothing can take my joy from me. My happiness is a daily choice. Regardless of what happens in my life, I choose my attitude, my outlook, and create my own happiness. I no longer wait around for it.

In 2014, I decided to get back into real estate as an entrepreneur and give it my best shot. I truly learned how to be a boss babe who could grow an enterprise. I partnered with one of my old bosses, and we grew a real estate team in Chicago and San Diego, where he relocated. One day I received a call from his wife, who never called me. She told me my partner had a stroke. In that moment, life got real. I realized how instantly and without warning life can change. This trauma was to make or break me.

My partner was expected to be in recovery for about two years as he learned a new normal, so I had to take over the business and run it on my own. To this day, I wonder how I did it, but it shows that we can do more than we believe we can. Working overtime while watching a man I admired face the most difficult challenge of his entire life was life-changing, humbling, and motivational. I decided my thoughts could determine my outcomes in life. If I didn't believe I could grow and manage a real estate team on my own, I couldn't. I had to overcome my limiting beliefs to determine what I could do in life.

I also had to surround myself with the right people. I

swallowed my pride and asked for help from those I knew were the best in the business. With their help, my clients were well taken care of so my partner could recover in peace.

A NEW DIRECTION

Then, like a lightbulb going off inside me, I decided to get back into investing, and become a life-and-business coach to give back to this wonderful real estate community. From that moment on, I dedicated my life to growing and creating the life I desired. A few years later, I decided to break my partnership and go out on my own.

Growing up Latina, with strong-minded parents in a strong-willed community, I had always made decisions based on what others wanted, or what I thought was the right thing to do. Now, I saw I had lived my life for others, not in my own truth. I had to trust in myself and what God placed in my heart about all areas of my life. I needed to stop worrying about what my family, friends, or colleagues would think and instead just be true to myself.

When life gets hard, it's time for you to ask yourself what you really want and if you are living the life you desire. During this time, I found myself married and in a toxic and painful union. Then I divorced and was single again. I also found myself in another failed relationship and had health issues that prevented me from having children.

Growing older and being a single and childless Latina was painful and made me feel like a failure. Latinas are often taught that we are valuable only if and when we got married and had children. If you don't, there must be something wrong with you, or you are too American and selfish. I had to accept myself and my value as a Latina, even though my culture viewed me otherwise.

I joined communities that did conscientious work and surrounded myself with like-minded and like-hearted people, especially women. This was the first time I truly became Danica. The freedom that came with this journey is inexplicable.

In 2022, I launched my own lifestyle brand that leans towards real estate, inspiration, and fun. I started my own real estate team, NFMS Group, created an investment business to start buying multi-units, and became a host for short-term rentals. I decided to get back into the dating world and take another chance on having a family. I am also writing my first book and coaching my first real estate students while traveling and living a life full of adventure.

This is truly who I am: a Latina from Humboldt Park, Chicago, going after her dreams and living in her truth. In the end, that is the best legacy you can leave behind—living powerfully in a space of complete authenticity, loving yourself and the world. It means not only growing and winning in life but giving the juice to others, so they can do the same for themselves. Then we can celebrate each other, side by side, Latinas to Latinas, showing the world that together we are better, stronger, and with our cultural passion and love, we can transform lives.

MY REAL ESTATE INSPIRATION

I didn't choose real estate; real estate chose me! Since I was a young child, architecture, finance, and customer service was a part of my world and made me feel alive. Real estate is so important in the Latino community because it is one of the best sources of building generational wealth and leaving a different legacy. With this advanced and modern world, we can have it all using real estate as a vehicle.

As you ponder a career in real estate, consider these questions:

1. Have you ever considered real estate as a vehicle to teach your children and grandchildren about building wealth?
2. Did you know that buying several multi-units over the course of ten years will not only create passive income but also increase your net worth year to year?
3. Are you prepared for retirement?
4. If retirement benefits are no longer available from the government, is the next generation prepared? What will happen to them?
5. What limiting beliefs do you have that are holding you back from having the financial life you desire?

BIOGRAPHY

Danica Matos has been in real estate for more than 15 years, wearing many hats ranging from broker to investor. She leads her own real estate team, NFMS Group.

Throughout her career, Danica has helped hundreds of families buy, sell, and invest in real estate. Born and raised in Chicago's Humboldt Park community, Danica's long-term goal is to help her community build generational wealth through real estate, especially in multi-family properties.

One of her proudest accomplishments was helping clients through the market crash of 2008. She coached many families out of their difficult financial situations with wise real estate advice, which gave those families a better future. Today, many are thriving and successful because of the real estate decisions they made at a critical time.

Danica believes that real estate is much more than just a business; it is a lifestyle that can serve as a vehicle to leave a legacy for your family. She hopes to impact her clients' lives by assisting them with every aspect of their real estate needs, from home ownership, to sales, to investment. She is regarded as a trusted life and business coach who can help families obtain the life they want.

Danica Matos
danica@nfmsgroup.com
Instagram: @nfmsdanica

MI DESTINO (MY DESTINY)

MARISOL FRANCO

"Everything I have learned in this business has translated into all other aspects of life."

As I reflect upon my career as a real estate professional, it's hard to believe that I have been in the field for eighteen years. It has been a financially rewarding career, but most importantly, it has given me a sense of purpose in life and the flexibility to raise and spend quality time with my two daughters. When they were born, I wanted to be a stay-at-home mom. Then when I made the choice to work in finance as a retail, commercial, lending, and retirement services officer, I quickly realized two things. First, I did not want to sacrifice being home for my daughters; and second, I needed a career that gave me more than just a paycheck. I wanted a career that was fulfilling, provided a sense of purpose, and offered the opportunity to engage and assist people with life-changing opportunities, like recruiting Latinos to become real estate agents or assisting them in buying their first home.

FROM AD TO AGENT

I discovered the real estate profession in 2004, when I came upon an ad in the *PennySaver*, my local newspaper. I remembered scrolling through a bunch of advertisements, coupons, and news articles, and then I saw the home listings and a real estate agent testimonial about a Latina woman who also was named Marisol. I immediately was inspired. *What if I could one day be the agent in the testimonial?* I began to challenge myself to envision a life-changing career in a field dominated by non-minority professionals. This epiphany changed my life forever, and I quickly acted upon it, based on the presence of a Latina in real estate who shared my name.

My discovery helped me realize three powerful things. First, the Latina community was grossly underrepresented in the real estate field. Second, my life's career work was to become a real estate professional tasked with bringing more Latinas into the profession; and third, through my job I could encourage and engage more Latino families to buy homes and realize the American dream.

I enjoyed being home raising my daughters, but I felt I lacked purpose. With the *PennySaver* in hand, I picked up the phone and called the brokerage firm in the ad to register for a class to earn my real estate sales license. I was determined to do well in the class and pass my licensure exam. I knew real estate would send me on a journey to become a better mom and member of my community. I was excited to begin my new career. Nearly two decades later, that same excitement is personified in my smile which dominates billboards of myself and advertises my real estate firm in my local area.

Eighteen years have passed in a mere blink of an eye, and I sometimes wonder where and who I would be if I had not seen that advertisement. At that point, I knew very little about real estate; only what I had learned through my experience in banking. However, I was prepared to overcome any barriers of entry into the field. I firmly believed this was my life's calling and nothing would stop me from succeeding.

MENTORS AND MILESTONES

When I began my career, white men dominated the field, particularly in the western Massachusetts area where I lived. I was one of roughly four Latinas selling real estate in the area. I had already overcome the most difficult hurdle—a mental one—by earning my license and accepting that I could be great in the real estate field, even coming from the Latino community.

My mother and late father, both immigrants from Puerto Rico, are my source of strength. They gave me a sense of pride, a strong work ethic, and most importantly, the belief that I could accomplish anything I wanted. I grew up with parents who had an indefatigable work ethic and worked two and three jobs to support me and my siblings. I had the genetics to keep pushing forward to achieve my goals.

When I started my career, brokerages didn't have developmental resources like teams and mentors to guide new agents towards success like they do today. Agents were all on their own, trying to make a name for themselves. My colleagues (who were also my competition) couldn't take the time to answer questions, share knowledge, and help ease me into this work. So, I took it upon myself to learn as much as I could, as quickly as possible, to get my business booming.

I started attending conferences where businessmen and women would speak to hundreds of eager individuals on real estate topics from marketing, to client retention, and to communication. I began reading books on entrepreneurship, business success stories, leadership, and real estate. I would contact those with experience to answer my questions and give me advice and guidance. By using these resources, I was able to quickly acquire a wealth of knowledge.

However, I knew that for myself, becoming successful the conventional way was not an option. I knew that I wasn't going to excel by following the same practices everyone else did. I had to stand out, and that meant to continuously keep learning and growing. Two role models who really made an impact in my business with their leadership skills were Veronica Figueroa and Tristan Ahumada.

I met Veronica at a National Association Hispanic Real Estate Professionals® (NAHREP) event in San Diego. I used to watch her motivational videos on YouTube, and I was so intrigued by her knowledge and drive. Her messages were so inspiring. I would tell myself I would meet her one day. My dream came true when I ran into her at the NAHREP event in San Diego, and we immediately connected! Years later, she is still my source of advice and motivation.

I learned about Tristan Ahumada through Facebook. He is the founder of Lab Coat Agents on Facebook, a private group of 150,000 real estate professionals. I attended my first Lab Coat conference in Miami in 2016. It was a turning point in my career. The elite group of top agents who presented a wealth of knowledge was a game changer for me. Tristan was one of the keynote speakers. I was attracted to his humility, leadership, and his passion for this business. Since then, he has remained a friend and a mentor who is always available. I'm truly thankful and blessed to have these two amazing role models in my life who continue guiding me and my team.

SUSTAINING SUCCESS

Real estate is a constantly changing business that requires adaptation to ensure success. However, this journey has taught me a couple of things that remain constant. Every day, I hear people discuss opportunities in real estate, including investment, sales, and development. Many believe real estate offers fast payout for minimal work. This is possible, but it takes hard work to sustain a career in this field.

One of the top three things I have learned to help maintain a long-term career in real estate is the importance of nurturing relationships. It's so easy to disconnect from past clients after completing a transaction, however it narrows your chances of them recommending your services to friends or family members or even reconnecting with you for themselves for another sales opportunity in the future. Nurturing past relationships may seem out of reach, overwhelming, or unnecessary, but doing so often guarantees repeat customers and referrals. Your effort can be as simple as sending holiday postcards, handwritten notes, a gift at the time of closing, or a phone call to check in and say, "Hello." When I get busy, this does not seem as important as fulfilling the needs of my current clients. However, the impact you can make on the recipient extends far beyond the gesture.

My second tip to success is to listen, not just hear. My late father always told me to "do good to others," which are words that I live by both personally and professionally. It is one thing to sit patiently while your client speaks and respond with what they would like to hear, but it is another to process what they are saying and respond constructively with their best interest in mind. As a young eager agent, I sometimes caught myself rushing through the steps of the sales process. At the end of the day, your transaction is only as successful as your client's satisfaction with the result—not just your commission check. For many people, the process leads to the purchase of their largest asset. It is vital that you hold their hand and guide them through it with empathy and patience. There will always be bumps along the road, but it is important that you always work towards a solution.

My third essential tip in business is to work with confidence. No matter your experience, it is important to remember that you were selected by your client for a reason. Confidence is the feeling or belief that one can rely on you for something and develop a firm trust in your knowledge. When you don't know the answer, it is important to let them know, and then find the answer for them.

When you are sure of what you know, it is vital that you assert your knowledge. Confidence stretches beyond your persona and your level of knowledge. It extends to defending your dedication to seek answers that you don't have and knowing the limits of your past experience and education.

I am so thankful that I took the leap into this business eighteen years ago. Real estate has provided well for me and my family and I am eternally grateful for it. Aside from motherhood, my career in real estate has been one of my most rewarding life journeys. I am recognized in the Top 50 Real Estate Teams Nationwide, as well as listed in the Top 100 Latino Agents in the United States and Puerto Rico by NAHREP. I have been honored to serve thousands of clients on their journey to home ownership, and have received many prestigious awards and been honored to be a panel speaker at many real estate conventions. I have met incredible role models and lifelong friends, and grown exponentially, both personally and professionally. I have supported my family and given back to my community. Above all, I have shown myself that "I can do this." I have found my sense of confidence and independence. My tireless hours of showings, open houses, research, studying, learning, and meetings have paid off and shaped me into the strong businesswoman I am.

In business, legacy is a term that references the success and impact you perpetuate when you are no longer on this Earth. For me, I hope that my legacy inspires those who I have touched in my line of work. I mentored the team members who joined me as my career progressed. When they came aboard, my goal was to provide the resources to them that I never had as a new agent. I transferred my experience and knowledge to these women and gave them a head start on their competition.

For my daughters, I hope that I have shown them that they can achieve anything they want with enough hard work. I hope they are paying attention to my tireless work ethic, my refusal to regard bumps in the road as boundaries, and the importance of independence and confidence in personal growth. For myself, everything I have learned in this business has translated into all other aspects of life. I share these life lessons with everyone so that they, too, can benefit from my growth and help inspire others. Stay true to your dreams, stay focused, and work hard to accomplish all of your goals.

MY REAL ESTATE INSPIRATION

I chose to become a realtor because I wanted a career that was fulfilling, provided a sense of purpose, and gave me an opportunity to engage and assist the Latino community with life-changing opportunities, like becoming real estate agents or buying their first home. I wanted to provide financial freedom for my family and have a flexible schedule to spend more time with my daughters. I wanted to be the go-to agent for all of my clients' real estate needs, and a leadership role model to young entrepreneurs and Latina businesswomen.

Do you have the drive and passion to be a real estate agent? Do you like helping people accomplish their home-buying goals? Are you available to work seven days a week in the beginning to build your business? Do you have a great support system that will encourage and help you? Do you have the leadership skills to listen, delegate, and help your clients with their real estate needs? If so, take the leap of faith and go for your dream. Team up with a good brokerage and find a mentor.

BIOGRAPHY

Marisol Franco has an undeniably strong presence and confidence that has propelled her into the rooms of some of the highest profile buyers and sellers in Massachusetts. She represents one of the most exciting developments underway in Wilbraham, Massachusetts—The Gardens of Wilbraham—a prestigious 55+ condo community.

A Massachusetts and Puerto Rican native, Marisol's professional career began in banking with TD Bank and MassMutual Financial Group before entering real estate. She has been named a Top 100 Latino agent by the National Association of Hispanic Real Estate Professionals® as well as in the Top 50 Real Estate Teams Nationwide, by her brokerage, which recently merged with Berkshire Hathaway Home Services Realty Professionals. She was featured in Top Agent Magazine and has done TV commercials. Her portfolio has recently expanded to include the greater Boston area, where she assisted her dear friend, Alex Cora, manager of the Boston Red Sox, with multiple transactions. She has since represented numerous noteworthy Red Sox players and coaches.

Marisol maintains a work-life balance by spending time with her family (especially her two daughters, Solimar and Carina), traveling, and watching her favorite baseball team, the Boston Red Sox.

Marisol Franco
marisolfrancorealtor@gmail.com
(413) 427-0151

OVERCOMING WITH GRATITUDE

TANYA DIAZ

"Life is a gamble. Always bet on yourself."

I grew up in a household full of strong women and one amazing man, my father. My parent's only son passed away at two months old. A year later, their "rainbow baby," me, Tanya (Quinones) Diaz, was born—the third daughter of four girls.

My parents are of Puerto Rican descent and raised us in the Logan Square neighborhood of Chicago. The neighborhood was infested with gangs and drugs, and a couple of times, our home was pierced with bullets while we slept. Unfortunately, we couldn't hide from it. We were exposed to it the second we opened our front door.

However, my parents did everything they could to protect us from the neighborhood and make us feel privileged. I never felt deprived of anything. Education and sports were important in our family. My sisters and I attended Catholic private grammar and high schools, and although I didn't appreciate it at the time, I realize now what a sacrifice it was for them to pay for our education.

FAMILY INSPIRATION

My father, Armando, worked for the city. During his off times, he would nurture his passion, which was real estate and construction. He was a self-taught contractor and would go on to become an investor and rehab his own properties. He inspired my love for real estate.

When most families were going out to dinner on the weekends, we would get in the car, get some Italian ice, and take a drive. We would leave our neighborhood and drive around affluent ones to admire the beautiful brick homes and mansions. My favorite homes had large windows without curtains so we could see inside. Some had beautiful baby grand pianos in the living room with colorful paintings. In others, you could see the exposed staircases that led to the second level. For my father, these were "rides around town," but I was inspired.

My mom, Miriam, is a tiny, but empowering Latina woman. She worked for the Chicago Public Schools as a teacher's aide and went on to become one of the city's best teachers. I had a front row ticket to watch my mother persevere. She held down a full-time job while she earned her bachelor's degree in education. She would leave her job, pick up me and my younger sister and take us to her night school classes. It wasn't until my adult years that I realized what a blessing all my parent's sacrifices were, and how they made me who I am today.

Growing up with three sisters wasn't easy. My sisters are beautiful, educated, strong women. In fact, my oldest sister is the bravest of the bunch. She served more than ten years in the military and is a retired U.S. staff sergeant from the U.S. Army. Let me tell you, they all set the bar really high.

THE RIGHT TIME FOR REAL ESTATE?

After high school, I attended Northeastern University, but every day I felt like there was more for me to do. I would daydream of being self-employed, because from a young age, I had always had a strong, entrepreneurial spirit. I did the typical lemonade stand, but I quickly realized that I could make money at family parties! I filled up garbage bags with the empty cans of soda and adult beverages, and the next day my dad took me to the facility where I could trade in the cans for cash. It was this spirit that led me to leave school and pursue real estate.

In 2002, I earned my real estate license. My fiancé (now my husband, David Diaz) was extremely supportive. For a few years, I worked in real estate part-time until we decided we wanted to grow our family. Also, as a wife, I made the decision to sideline real estate to support my husband in reaching his goals and childhood dream. David is a 1996 U.S. Boxing Olympian and by the many sacrifices we made together, he is a former World Boxing Council Lightweight Champion of the World. David had an amazing career that blessed us with great experiences and beautiful memories. He fought on HBO in the biggest arenas in Las Vegas, at the highest level of the sport. We were surrounded by many of his fans, reporters, lights, and cameras. Putting my goals on hold was worth it. Then in 2011, after all the blood, sweat, and (my) tears, David hung up his gloves for the final time.

By then, we had three sons. Sometimes as wives and mothers, we naturally tend to care for everyone else before ourselves. In 2013, my youngest son was four and I found myself wanting to pursue my own goals and finally put myself first. I was missing real estate, but I had let my license elapse. I registered for classes and became licensed again, but it was not as easy this time around. I studied at home while bouncing my four-year-old on my lap, helping my two other little ones with their school assignments, and simultaneously cooking dinner. Some days I doubted myself. I wasn't sure if I would be able to accomplish what I had before. I knew that quitting wasn't an option—it never is. The challenges were a beautiful reminder of my, "why," and my "why" in 2013 had become bigger and more meaningful than it was in 2002.

After earning my license, I joined an office as a real estate broker and within a few short years, I earned my managing broker's license. Then I also was allowed to manage, guide, mentor, grow, and oversee transactions done by other Realtors. I met amazing people and learned from some of the best. Soon David was inspired to go into real estate, too, and I became his managing broker.

AN ATTITUDE OF GRATITUDE

Sometimes life throws you a curveball. For some time, I had been feeling sick, and not like myself. I scheduled a doctor's appointment and after a few tests, I was diagnosed with stage II kidney disease—IgA nephropathy, or Berger's disease. To say I was devastated was an understatement. I cried in fear, because I had seen other family members suffer with kidney disease. The day I received the news, I was sitting on the front porch of our home with my husband. He hugged me and told me I was going to be okay. I allowed myself to experience the emotions for just that one day. I've never been one to throw a "pity party" for myself. I believe in God, and I knew that He had big plans for me.

Instead of feeling sorry for myself, I turned my emotions into an attitude of gratitude. I'm alive! I come from a family of women who are resilient warriors. My grandmothers were my greatest inspirations, and had endured much but always remained strong and kept pushing forward. I couldn't let them down. Since that diagnosis, I feel great, my kidneys are still good, and I am enjoying life one day at a time.

In 2018, I felt another calling in my heart—I wanted to open my own brokerage. After I spoke with my husband, I called my best friend, Jannette, and shared my plan. Sometimes you need a voice of reassurance and reasoning, and she's definitely that voice for me. I knew I was ready to take that leap of faith, and in September, we established the Main Event Real Estate Group.

My intention was to only work alongside my husband, but

what the Lord had planned for me was bigger. Don't you just love when that happens?! In a few short months, we went from a team of two to fourteen, with no recruiting. I lived my passion for helping others achieve their goals, and loved seeing our team win! There were challenges, and times when we beat ourselves down and suffered from imposter syndrome, but when you're going after your goals, you only need validation from within.

LIVING LIFE, GIVING BACK

Soon afterwards, I joined the board of directors for the Chicago chapter of the National Association of Hispanic Real Estate Professionals® (NAHREP). Its mission of advancing sustainable Hispanic homeownership was extremely important to me. Being on the board allowed us to help fulfill the mission of educating and empowering our real estate peers. I personally felt empowered by the support and knowledge of the other directors who also were a part of NAHREP Chicago. The relationships you build within the organization are priceless. If you're in the real estate profession, I encourage you to connect with NAHREP and be a part of an organization that educates Latinos and does so much more than we can do alone.

When my two-year term on the board ended, I knew I wanted to continue to give back to the community. When I'm not wearing my real estate hat, I switch it for a baseball cap. It's no secret that my two favorite baseball players are my sons, David (seventeen) and Elias (fifteen), and my favorite artist is my son, Silas (thirteen). As a mother of three teenage boys living in a town fueled with gun violence, I know it's extremely important to keep them busy. So, when my husband approached me about partnering with some friends to create The Clubhouse, I was all for it.

The Clubhouse is a facility in the Belmont Cragin community of Chicago that focuses on baseball/softball training and builds better athletes, both mentally and physically. The doors are open every day to youth who use this as their safe haven. They spend countless hours at the facility. In the evenings, you'll find women empowering women during intense workout classes. We were helping to build a stronger community with safer neighborhoods and giving back. And I believe you can have all the success and accomplishments in the world, but it means nothing if you haven't given back.

Recently, I lost three important people in my life within twelve months: my grandmother, Mama; Ariana, one of my hustle-driven agents; and my father-in-law, who lived with us. We should always expect the unexpected. Yet when life knocks you down, you have to build the strength and courage to get back up. Despite the challenges, don't lose focus, and stay motivated and driven.

I'm proud that I've followed in my parent's footsteps and currently own multiple properties with the goal of continuing to build my real estate portfolio. Aside from my family, my motivation comes from our team at Main Event Real Estate. They continue to push me to become a better version of myself, every single day. Remember that life is a gamble. Always bet on yourself.

MY REAL ESTATE INSPIRATION

I chose real estate because from a young age, I saw my parents invest, rehab, and rent properties. I saw their passion and the excitement of tenants who were delighted with their remodeled apartments. From then on, I was inspired.

There are many different paths within real estate. I've been able to purchase and rent properties, train and educate real estate professionals as a designated managing broker, host women empowerment events, sit as a director on the largest Hispanic real estate board, and open my own real estate brokerage.

I get to enjoy a career that I'm passionate about. The beauty of real estate is that you never stop learning. You're a problem solver, and you get to meet and connect with people and be a part of life-changing experiences for clients. No two days are ever the same, and I wouldn't change it for anything.

For anyone interested in a career in real estate, look into your local real estate association or real estate schools. Real estate can be challenging, but the reward is beyond measure. Silence any doubt from within and go for it. You can do it!

BIOGRAPHY

Tanya Diaz was born and raised in the Logan Square neighborhood in Chicago. She has worked in real estate for more than ten years, and is passionate about the industry. Tanya is the designated managing broker/owner of Main Event Real Estate Group, which she opened in 2018.

Tanya was recently featured in Top Agent Magazine and has been a host and speaker at women empowerment events. She is committed to inspiring the next generation of strong, Latina women to have a voice for themselves and accomplish their life goals. She also has served as past executive secretary for the Chicago chapter of the National Association of Hispanic Real Estate Professionals® (NAHREP), and continues to support the mission of The Clubhouse, a facility owned by her husband and friends to develop strong minds and talent through sports training and exercise.

Tanya understands being part of a champion team. She is the mother of three boys and wife of 1996 U.S. Olympian and former Lightweight World Champion, David Diaz. Now she surrounds herself with a winning team of real estate professionals daily.

When not in a real estate deal, Tanya enjoys traveling, photography, spending time with family and being a baseball mom.

Tanya Diaz
TANYA@maineventrealestate.com
Facebook: tanya.quinonesdiaz

FIGURING IT OUT

TINA MARIE HERNANDEZ

"When I finally recognized that I am the only one who can make ME happy, my life changed."

"Mom, I'm home. Thanks for making lunch," I'd say, coming through the door from school. But there was no lunch and my mom was not home. Pretending made me feel less lonely. The reality was that I was a teenage latchkey kid who made their own lunch and had learned to be self-sufficient.

My parents only had two children, my brother and me. They divorced when I was two, and my father remarried and had other children. My brother stayed with our dad, while I spent most of my time with my mother. I often felt like an only child. I knew my mom worked hard to provide a good life for me and I was grateful, but it affected me. My schoolwork suffered. I wouldn't do my homework, barely went to class, and would skip school to hang out with my friends. Believe it or not, we'd go look at fancy houses and neighborhoods, and I would dream of living there.

I began dating a real estate professional, who worked with my mother. He was older and had a career, a home, and a nice car, which at the time, met my definition of success. We had our first child, my oldest daughter, when I was eighteen. The relationship was unhealthy, but I kept trying to make it work because I wanted that fantasy home life. As I tried to save the relationship, I had my first son. It didn't fix anything, but his birth made me realize I didn't want to raise my children in that environment, so I left. I was twenty years old. I moved into my father's converted garage. It was tough living there; he had my brothers and my sisters, and I did not want to burden him with my kids.

EVERYTHING AND NOTHING

The saving grace in my situation was that I had passed my real estate exam and had a mom in real estate to show me the business. I joined her firm and leaned on her expertise. I was the first rookie agent and nobody took me seriously. Yet I was determined to provide a different life for my kids. That white-picketed fence was going to be ours if I had to cut the damn tree down and build it myself!

My father worked in construction and had a partner who was smart, nice, and interested in me. After three years of dating, we got married and he took my two children in as his own. When I was 25, we moved into my dream neighborhood. It was the kind you see on television, filled with tree-lined streets, and huge houses boasting big backyards. It was the same neighborhood that my friends and I would drive around when we skipped school. I had always visualized myself living there, hosting family gatherings, and my kids attending the neighborhood school. I had put it out into the universe and my vision came true!

My husband also had a real estate license. Together, we started a small independent real estate office. I was still in my early twenties and trying hard to live up to who I thought I had to be in this relationship. I thought I had to be firm and do it all. We had two children together, but I didn't want him to feel responsible for my older two children, so I continued to work so my kids would never be a financial burden.

I also felt lost in this marriage. He came from a stable family and was one of nine children. His parents still were married and in love. That was everything I wanted for me and my family, but I never realized it would cost me my identity.

NEW OPPORTUNITIES

In 2008, after sixteen years of marriage, we divorced. I left with nothing except my integrity and my smile. I knew that I would figure it out.

I rented a place near the kid's school. It was expensive, so I had to be resourceful. At times I didn't have money for food or gas, so when I took my kids to school, I would stay at another mom's house nearby until school let out. That way I would save gas by not having to travel back and forth. I would also find ways to invite myself to dinner by cooking for them. Little did she know I could barely feed my own kids.

Soon after, I started working for Century 21 as an office manager but was still a licensed Realtor. It was the beginning of the 2008 market crash. When the market turned, I noticed where it was headed. There were a lot of institutional listings that were real estate owned (REO). I told my boss that we should attend a conference to acquire some. Surprisingly, he agreed with me, and we booked our trip. I wanted to attend with him because I knew he would be a big presence in that very male-dominated segment of the real estate game.

Once at the conference, I learned that he wasn't including me in any of the meetings he was taking. I didn't like that. Institutional accounts stay with the broker, not the agent, and he was the broker. If I was going to be slaving away getting business for him, he needed to be a team player!

I did have my broker's license but had never used it. Sitting in my kid's bedroom while they were away with their dad, I decided to take a leap of faith. I thought if I didn't do it now, all of my hard work would go to another man, and I just couldn't let that happen again. I needed to find my voice, stand my ground, and do this for myself.

I was still trying to navigate through my not-yet-finalized divorce, as well as raising kids on my own. My oldest daughter had graduated from high school and was in college. I didn't know how I was going to pay for it, but I knew it was non-negotiable. Once again, my thought was that I would figure it out. My oldest son was a senior in high school and my two younger ones were in private Catholic school. I wondered how I was even thinking of opening my own company when I had to dodge the lady at my kid's school who collected the tuition payments.

But I knew investing in my company was just as important. I had to attend those REO conferences if I was going to turn my livelihood around. With my other expenses, I couldn't afford to go to the conferences, so I decided to move in with my aunt. With the savings in rent, I could get to those conferences and land those listings. However, when I attended my first one, alone and nervous, I quickly found out I was a small fish in a bowl of bigger, more experienced fish.

I remember calling my best friend. When I admitted I was still in my hotel room she smacked me around a lil'. She told me to get out, put on a smile, and do what I do best—make friends with people. She was right. I needed to find the security I had lost and claim it. Not just for me, but for my kids who were at home waiting for me.

So, I went to the lobby bar, where all the big connections are made, and did "me." I was so green on how to network that when I did meet an asset manager, I handed him a resume with all of my accomplishments. I will never forget how hard he laughed at me, but he gave me a shot. That "shot" was an hour and a half away, but I accepted it to get established and gain credibility. And I worked it!

AT THE READY

With opportunity, you have to be ready and know what you're doing. Just because you are given an opportunity doesn't mean you didn't earn it, but I knew I had a lot to learn about servicing the REO market, and I had to find ways to educate myself. I learned about an organization called the National Association of Hispanic Real Estate Professionals®. (NAHREP). Their mission was to educate and empower the Hispanic real estate professional, like me.

I joined NAHREP, attended some events, and volunteered on the local board as the educational director. I needed to get educated and what better way to do that than through the resources of NAHREP? I learned what I needed from the speakers that I would bring on. It was perfect for me!

Through it all, I never second-guessed myself and I believed everything was going to work out. I visualized what I wanted, including my company, and I prepared for opportunities. I was getting more listings, but not more money. Then I heard that the U.S. Department of Housing and Urban Development (HUD) was looking for a local agent, and I actually knew someone who worked there. I put my best foot forward and out of 3,500 applicants, I was one of three who landed the job. Being accepted didn't mean the flood gates of listing would open, but it did mean that you needed to be ready if it happened. So, with only two hundred dollars in my account and a credit card, I bought thirty "for sale" signs and all of the other custom signs HUD requested. Then, I waited.

My oldest son had since graduated from high school and was helping me with my company. I also was blessed to have my best friend by my side helping me as well. I called my first company meeting. We read and reread all the specific instructions on how to manage a HUD listing so we would be ready.

After that, things really did change. We became successful, but the biggest blow of my life came when my dad passed away in 2011. I lost my biggest cheerleader. My person. I fell into a deep depression but didn't let anyone see it. I had to keep it together and keep moving forward because I still had care for my babies. I really leaned into my family and began a more spiritual journey. I learned how to really find happiness within myself. When I finally recognized that I am the only one who can make ME happy, my life changed. My relationship with my kids and people around me changed, too. I also felt ready to find someone and share my life.

OPPORTUNITY TOGETHER

I sat down and wrote out a list of the characteristics that I wanted in a man. I also became more involved with NAHREP as the Orange County chapter president. I then worked my way to national coach and became a regional co-chair. I always say I am a product of NAHREP. This association opened so many doors for me. I've met so many amazing friends that I now consider family. Of course, the biggest connection I made at NAHREP was my wonderful husband . . . the man who checks all of the boxes on my list.

Together we are building an amazing real estate company where we teach agents about investing as well as work/life balance. We have fixed and flipped a couple dozen homes. However, our biggest real estate adventure has been purchasing rental properties to help us with our retirement.

When I realized we were priced out of the rental market in Southern California where I live, I started to look out of state for rentals. My husband and I became owners of nearly twenty rental properties. These properties have helped put my children through college and will give our grandchildren the "Latino Leg Up," as I like to call it. Meanwhile, I can enjoy what is important to me—my children and my family. They are a constant reminder that tomorrow is not promised and that opportunity is just around the corner for them. Just like it was for me!

MY REAL ESTATE INSPIRATION

Real estate is all I know. It has now become my passion. I like to call myself "The Real Estate Whisperer." I look at a house and can envision it in its highest form. That could be as a rental, a larger place with additional square footage, a short-term rental, or a dream home for a single family.

My husband tells me I haven't worked a day in my life because I do what I love. I challenge you to do the same thing. What is your passion? It doesn't have to be real estate, but if that is what you know, it can be a vehicle to get you to your passion. At the end of the day, it's about controlling your happiness. That is the only way you can be the best you for yourself and the ones you love.

Things that help me control my happiness are meditation and spending time with my family. FOCUS ON THINGS YOU CAN CONTROL!

BIOGRAPHY

Tina Marie Hernandez is celebrating her thirtieth year in the real estate industry. She has earned success with her clients and peers by understanding the importance of creating "win-win" scenarios for all parties involved in any market. She is well known for supporting community efforts that are designed to bring opportunities for affordable first-time homeownership, as well as the sale and purchase of fine homes and estates.

Her efforts in helping the community have earned her positions with the local and national leadership of the National Association for Hispanic Real Estate Professionals®. With this organization she is able to empower other professionals in her industry to succeed and make a difference in their businesses.

Tina and her husband, Rich Hernandez, have built a thriving independent real estate company but felt they needed a partner. In 2020, during the pandemic, they took the leap and partnered with Coldwell Banker to bring a luxury brand to their diverse market.

Tina's proudest accomplishment is her family. In her spare time, she is busy being a grandma and enjoying her four beautiful children and her grandchildren. They help her remember that tomorrow is not promised, and everyone should cherish the gift of today.

Tina Marie Hernandez
Tina.marie@cbomnigroup.com
Instagram: @Tinamarie_hernandez

A LEAP OF FAITH

SHEYLA PADILLA

"Real estate is financial freedom."

There are two important essentials in life: housing and food. All my life I was determined to provide one of them as a way to live out my purpose. It was quite a journey to get to my career in real estate! I was born in Bayamon, Puerto Rico, on February 29, which was leap day of that year. It makes complete sense since I became someone who was always willing to take a leap!

When I was an infant, my mother decided to leave the tropical island and move to Chicago, Illinois, for a better life. I was raised in the Humboldt Park community where I attended elementary school. Spanish was my first language, and classrooms were separated into Spanish and English. Growing up, I never felt like I fit in because of the language barrier. Then, just before I completed the third grade, I asked my mom to enroll me in the

English-speaking classroom. She agreed. There I faced academic difficulties, but it was my first big leap. Being fluent in two languages would eventually prove to be my advantage as a Latina in real estate.

ADVENTURES IN INVESTMENT PROPERTIES

One of my first jobs out of school was working for an international financial institution as a compliance analyst. It was the position that molded me into a young, Latina professional. The superiors valued my ideas and respected my work ethic. I was exposed to the corporate world and prepared for my entry into real estate. It blessed me with the opportunity to become financially independent, save for retirement, understand the value of a dollar, respect the power of credit, and most importantly, learn how to mitigate risk. I recall picking the brains of individuals on the trading floor about what markets offered the best return on investment. "Real estate" was the answer I heard most.

My love for real estate began in the summer of 2005. I purchased my first three-flat property in Chicago's Austin neighborhood. It was a definite leap because I became a homeowner and landlord overnight with absolutely no training, education, or experience.

In the fall of 2007, I purchased a new construction condo in Chicago's up-and-coming East Garfield Park community. I purchased there because of the gentrification and steadfast economic development of the area. The exclusive rooftop access had the most incredible view of the city's downtown skyline, and the Fourth of July was one of my favorite times of the year there. I had the best seat in the house to see the panoramic fireworks show, and I have fond memories of being there with family and friends.

Weeks after my condo purchase, I learned that my employer was negotiating one of the biggest acquisitions in finance history. It was settled just before the financial crisis and proved to be one of the greatest failures by a chief executive officer (CEO). In the spring of 2010, I was furloughed from a career I loved. Six years in the finance industry yielded a positive return on my investment of time. Leaving was bittersweet.

That same year, the three-flat investment property began experiencing turnover and problematic residents who were violating the terms of their lease. They caused a lot of stress and chaos. It was evident they were taking advantage of my inexperience. I didn't know how to enforce the leases, nor did I retain legal counsel to understand my rights as a landlord. The basement flooded three times in one year, and the damage was not covered by the insurance company. It was a sewer back-up issue, which was an exclusion on the policy I didn't know about. I had to pay for the flood control system and repairs out of my own pocket. My first investment property turned out to be a nightmare money pit.

Meanwhile, my primary residence was experiencing roof issues. Water was coming through the can lights when it rained. I was unemployed and losing everything I had, and I knew I needed to make some difficult and uncomfortable decisions if I was going to survive.

I faced a lot of adversity in real estate and often thought of quitting it completely. However, during my healing process after losing everything, I took the initiative to educate myself on the municipal, county, state and federal laws that govern housing. I had a landlord consultation with a real estate attorney who I eventually had on my speed-dial.

I pressed on, but in the fall of 2013, the three-flat was just not profitable anymore. I did a short sale on it and a deed-in-lieu on the condo to avoid foreclosure. I was heartbroken and felt like a complete failure.

A PURPOSEFUL OPPORTUNITY

In the summer of 2015, I was approached by a long-term investor and trusted friend with a real estate business proposition. It was the perfect opportunity to turn my pain into power. I was asked to spearhead a residential investment portfolio and scale the business. It was time to leap again!

The new position gave me the ability to revisit my purpose. Providing quality housing and healthy living in Chicago's communities instantly became a top priority. It was my chance to lead with passion and confidence. I was determined to establish success beyond my imagination.

Through my tenure, I developed, tested, and deployed winning systems and procedures. I created an effective business plan, an annual budget and cost analysis, and reduced unnecessary expenses. I introduced the operations management system input/output transformation model and reporting, identified the strengths and weaknesses of the business with tools, such as a strategic framework used to assess the political, economic, social, technological, environmental, and legal factors (PESTEL analysis), financial modeling, business model canvas, and feasibility reporting. I also implemented a compliance framework and set internal and external controls for risk management. The efforts paid off and the company grew to become a healthy brand.

Throughout the years, we purchased distressed properties through the multiple listing service (MLS), live auctions, off-market, and tax deeds. We would then renovate, rent, refinance, and repeat. We followed the buy, renovate, rent, refinance, and repeat method (BRRRR) to perfection. To date, we have renovated thirty-four properties and sold nineteen throughout Chicago and the neighboring suburbs.

Being a Latina in real estate is a dream come true. I have revolutionized the way construction is defined in a male-dominated industry. I am determined to cut through red tape and continue earning my stripes. It's not always deals in heels; I get my hands dirty, too! I have a pink construction hard hat, pink steel toe boots, and pink tools. Walking through the job sites is always gratifying.

I recognized that in order to keep the well-oiled machine running, I needed to obtain my real estate broker's license. In the summer of 2017, I successfully passed the exam. I was ecstatic and ready to break records. In the spring of 2018, I received an award from the Chicago Association of Realtors® for Top Neighborhood Producer Units Sold—West Garfield Park. In the spring of 2020, I went on to receive two awards from the Chicago Association of Realtors® for Top Neighborhood Producer Volume Sold and Top Neighborhood Producer Units Sold in North Lawndale. Those awards hang proudly in my home office.

BUILDING FOR THE FUTURE

Failing in real estate nearly a decade ago started me on a path to success. I was able to adjust my crown, reevaluate my optimism, and reignite the notion that anything is possible as long as I believe in myself.

Failure also was an essential part of my growth. With each leap, I learned from each trial and error. Learning to delegate, however, was the final obstacle I had to overcome. As a strong and independent Latina, I am accustomed to doing everything on my own, so trust for the rest often comes slowly.

In February 2021, I hired an assistant. That was the beginning of re-examining my role as a business owner. I knew that if I was going to have adequate support, I needed to invest my time in training her appropriately. I took six months off, and committed them to my assistant, who I am blessed to have. She is a bilingual Latina, fluent in Spanish, and a breath of fresh air to my day-to-day operations. She brings balance to my auto-pilot days and has an enormous amount of patience. Those six months were a valuable investment. She's a fortunate young lady who is learning all of my secrets and golden nuggets.

My team and I also are renovating our biggest project to date, Project Penny with approximately 10,000 square feet.

The mixed-use property boasts six residential units and two commercial spaces. Project Penny is going to be a milestone in my real estate career and the home of my future office.

A significant part of my success and growth is due to my business partner, the long-term investor and trusted friend, whom I call my work husband. He is my confidant and always keeps me motivated. He reminds me of my strengths as a Latina in the construction industry and defines me as the First Lady of the crew. His talent and multi-tasking skills on the field are impressive. His continuous support and guidance mean everything to me.

I had aspired to create a lifelong legacy by building generational wealth. My newfound passion is to invest in different markets, including international ones, when Project Penny is complete. My family and friends call me a workaholic. I don't think I'm a workaholic. I think that I started my business the unconventional way and I am never content with its current state. I believe that in order to achieve an optimal level you have to invest the time and energy.

While I do find myself working late nights and occasionally on Saturdays, I am a firm believer in balance and taking time off to recharge and connect with other things that bring me joy. In January 2022, I made a decision to take Sundays off and rest because health is wealth. No amount of currency can replace me and my mental health is extremely important. I take it so seriously that my office will have a wellness room, which is a private area where an employee or contractor can escape if they are feeling unwell, stressed, or have a maternal necessity. It will provide a vital break from others in the open spaces of the office. Since stress affects the body in a number of harmful ways from migraines to weight problems and more, that brief reprieve can help keep the well-being of my employees and contractors in check. Maintaining a healthy work environment and creating a culture of safety and security is part of my brand and a perpetual goal.

Seventeen years after I got my start in real estate, I am blessed to be the CEO of my company. I am providing jobs and quality apartments, while selling turnkey properties.

My words of advice to Latinas interested in real estate would be to exercise patience in everything you do. Building a brand takes time. Renovations do not happen in an hour like they do on HGTV. Education, resources, support, and experience are all vital to succeeding in real estate. Rushing into an investment property without the proper tools or financial resources is a formula for disaster.

Finally, surround yourself with like-minded individuals and you will organically elevate yourself. By joining strong community groups and local councils, you will network and grow.

Real estate is financial freedom. It is the number one strategy for bridging the wealth gap. It is the master key that unlocks many doors. It is a solid foundation to fostering long-term business relationships. It will allow you the flexibility to realize one of the world's most important mottos: work to live, don't live to work. Real estate is a trusted resource for living life on your own terms, and the oldest and proven method to building generational wealth.

MY REAL ESTATE INSPIRATION

I am inspired by the work of others from inside and outside of the real estate industry. These books have kept me aligned and focused, and I recommend them to any aspiring Latina real estate professional!

- *Maximizing Personal Wealth* by Russ Alan Prince, Hannah Shaw Grove, Carlo A. Scissura, and Frank W. Seneco. The book with the secret sauce. A must have on your bookshelf as a business owner. It is loaded with information on how to position yourself for success and preserve it.
- *Who Moved My Cheese?* by Spencer Johnson, MD. An excellent book about change. To be effective, one must be open to adapting to new ideas. In the story, the characters are faced with unexpected change in their search for the cheese. One of them eventually deals with change successfully and writes what he has learned on the maze walls for you to discover.
- *HBR's 10 Must Reads on Emotional Intelligence* by Daniel Goleman. This is one of my favorite books. As the CEO of my company, leading a team of employees, contractors, and vendors can be overwhelming. This book enabled me to stay centered, focused, and become a better listener.

I also recommend these real estate, financial guidance, self-help, and health podcasts:

- *Straight Up Chicago Investor*
- *Suze Orman's Women & Money*
- *WorkLife with Adam Grant*
- *The HEAL Podcast*

Best wishes in your real estate pursuits!

BIOGRAPHY

Sheyla Padilla is a bilingual, seasoned investor in Chicago with a mission to shatter glass ceilings and promote social equity. For seventeen years, she has been successful in real estate acquisitions and sales, project and business management, construction, and interior design.

Sheyla is the CEO of a construction company and a woman and minority-owned, licensed general contractor. She meticulously renovates distressed properties, holds them as investments, or sells the assets on the market. Her strong leadership, listening and communication skills, attention to detail, and organization are the core values to the business.

With a firm belief that quality apartments and healthy living are a right, not a privilege, Sheyla heads the operations of a residential and commercial leasing company. She oversees an investment portfolio of fourteen properties in Chicago's west and south side communities. She successfully grew the company by perfecting the real estate investor's BRRRR method.

When she is not making executive decisions, Sheyla enjoys traveling and spending quality time with family and close friends. She is an avid herbal tea drinker and follows the paleo diet. She loves listening to music and has a fond appreciation for nature, particularly flowers and plants.

Sheyla Padilla
Instagram: @iamsheylapadilla
Facebook: @SheylaPadilla
LinkedIn: Sheyla Padilla

THE FALLING DREAM

BAXTIE RODRIGUEZ

"Repeatedly, I have faced challenge and kept moving forward. I have learned to never give up and never forget to look up."

I was born to hardworking parents in Chicago's Humboldt Park area. As a child, I remember my father working two jobs so me and my three siblings could go to school and live comfortably.

Despite all my parents did for us, life wasn't easy. My dad worked at a factory during the day and headed to another job at night. He would take my sisters and me to his second job, so we had little social life. My mother stayed busy on the second shift and also was not home often, although she would never forget to leave us a nice, warm meal.

At one time, all six of us crowded into a tiny apartment that my father rented, behind a grocery store on Augusta Boulevard. To make ends meet, we would sell canned goods, boxed goods, and candy to our neighbors. My dad would deliver pizza or drive an ice cream truck. At one time, he even opened a burger-and-hot-dog place.

In retrospect, I can see how much their daily sacrifices did for us. They taught me how to work hard, thrive, and overcome any challenge. For vacations, we would drive somewhere and stay at a Yogi Bear's Jellystone Park Camp-Resorts Campground because it was cheaper than staying at a hotel. My parents struggled without complaint and pushed themselves to their absolute limit to put food on the table.

Throughout their sacrifices and bravery, I was no angel. No matter how much they did for me, I wanted more. I saw my parents work long hours and wondered why there was not enough money to go around. I was very rebellious and thought I knew everything. As an unsatisfied teenager, I ran away on multiple occasions. Every time, my family came after me.

Then, I became a teenage mom. I dropped out of high school. From there, I had no choice. I had to make it work on my own. I had to survive. Failure, as the saying goes, was not an option.

SURVIVAL AND THE FIRST DREAM

In time, I got my act together. I went back to school, graduated, and found a job in the corporate world. It all seemed *perfect* to me—until I became single again. At thirty years old, I was raising three young children on my own.

Then, everything fell apart. I lost my job, my car, and the

mortgage bills were piling up. My checking account was empty. But to feed my kids, I would write checks at the Jewel grocery store, knowing they would bounce. I would pay them back, plus the small bounce fee, as soon as I could write a good check. I did this repeatedly. It was an act of survival until things got better.

This was when the *falling dream* first met me in my sleep.

In the dream, I am running up a hill. It's nighttime. In the darkness, I see a four-foot-tall wrought iron fence, spanning the gap between two mountains. There is a high cliff atop each mountain. Unsure whether I should climb over the fence or run into it, I feel myself *falling*. I am barreling face down off the cliff. My eyes, wide-open, barely pierce the darkness. I can't stop staring at the never-ending fall. Fear, loneliness, and an overwhelming cold wash over me.

SOMETHING DIFFERENT

I knew what that dream meant, and I knew I had to do something about it. My uncle's wife, who came to live with my parents when I was a troubled teenager, was my inspiration. She came to Chicago from Puerto Rico at the age of forty-two. Speaking little English, she took a job in real estate, and a short time later, she was a top-producing real estate professional.

Here was something different—an example I could follow. I thought she was intelligent and elegant. She also went from sleeping in my parent's spare room to buying her own home in the suburbs. She proved that anyone could quickly change their life situation. I decided I would do the same but skip the real estate license and get my managing broker's license instead.

Of course, the first year was difficult. Learning real estate takes time. As my unemployment benefits dwindled and child support was hardly making a dent in the bills, I had to sell my home and decide on my next move.

With the money from selling my home, I purchased a 700-square-foot, two-bedroom, one-bathroom condo on Harlem Avenue in the Montclair area. The home needed some work, but there was no mortgage payment, which meant I could stretch my meager savings farther to make cosmetic repairs on the kitchen and the living room. When I worked on the bedrooms, the kids and I moved into the living room.

Not long after wrapping up the remodel, a friend of mine visited, told me she loved what I had done with the place, and made me an offer on the spot. My $65,000 investment was now a $135,000 property, only four months later.

That was when I met another version of myself: the house-flipper.

Using the funds from that flip, I purchased a more suitable home for my four-person family and remodeled it for security. If all else failed, I knew I could flip it and make a profit.

Then, I launched my own real estate brokerage out of my basement while renting a virtual office to appear professional. Gradually, I recruited twelve agents and an administrative team. We worked out of my basement until I was able to rent an office space on Addison Street near Harlem Avenue in Chicago.

RETURN OF THE FALLING DREAM

Everything was incredible. I was a top producer, as were my agents. We were flipping homes, producing multi-unit properties, and collaborating with investors on bigger and better deals. I started to earn more money than I ever dreamed. My kids were by my side, and I was thriving.

Then, the 2008 economic crisis hit, and it all came tumbling down. The party was over. Twelve agents, four administrators, and 65 short-sale files—they were all on my shoulders. The banks couldn't help. The agents depended on me for deals, and their clients blamed me for the crash. Before long, I was short on payroll. I thought about my kids. How was I going to take care of them?

The falling dream returned. That cliff of darkness appeared regularly, and I felt scared, alone, and cold all over again. In the dream, I would say, "Please God, let me hit the bottom, so I can bounce back up."

Over the next two years, I depleted my savings to keep my business afloat and support my children. Then, I had to close my doors, facing total insolvency. I was embarrassed to face my agents. I sent them all FedEx envelopes with a letter explaining what was happening.

I was facing foreclosure. I cashed out my 401(k) retirement fund and pawned the few pieces of jewelry that I owned. When that money ran out, I filed for bankruptcy and sent my children to live with their father so I could plan a way forward.

The economy was still in shambles, but I figured I could still flip houses. I asked my father to partner with me and he agreed to fund me and my sister for some projects.

The hours were long. My sister and I worked incessantly, looking to buy and sell short sales. I managed the transactions, she purchased materials, and we managed our crew together, rehabbing one property at a time. One short sale cost us a mere $17,000; we rehabbed it with $40,000 of budget and sold it for $130,000. We took the $73,000 profit and divided by three. We felt we were on to something.

Nobody knew it, but I was practically homeless during that period of my life. I slept inside homes that I was remodeling. None of it made sense, and I felt deeply confused. Despite my hard work, I was still struggling.

Then, one evening on one of those ratty mattresses that had become my home, I watched the movie *Eat, Pray, Love* alongside my brother. The movie engrossed me, and my brother noticed. "I think someone is taking a trip soon," he remarked.

He was right. Scraping together whatever money I could, I purchased an airline ticket to Bali, Indonesia, and found a home stay for $400 per month. My life was about to take yet another turn.

LIVING HUMBLY, LOOKING UP

I spent a month in Bali with a young woman and her three children who took in travelers to help make ends meet. Her husband was absent, and the village was poor. Accommodations were *very* basic.

Every day the family would meet in the living room—a patch outside the home—to watch TV and eat meals. The menu was rice and chicken twice per day plus bananas for snacks. I helped the mother pick lice out of her little girls' long, beautiful hair. No one owned more than one pair of shoes and they rotated through three outfits. The mother didn't own a car, just a scooter. Every day was a struggle.

Despite it all, I felt the *love*. They were strangers, but they welcomed me happily. They were grateful for their simple life and would pray and offer thanks every morning. During one of those morning prayers, a new feeling came to me: *shame*. I was with people who were happy with very little. I was privileged, yet filled with self-pity. Even traveling to another country to figure myself out was a privilege.

I had the falling dream one last time while I was in Bali. This time was different. It was still dark, and the hill was the same. Once again when I fell off the cliff, I asked God, "Why won't I hit the bottom and bounce back up?" This time, I heard a reply.

"Look up."

I did and there, above me, was a bright light in a vivid blue sky. The sunshine was *spectacular*. It was beautiful—the air and the warmth—and I breathed deeply and easily.

Finally, I thought to myself.

I realized I had never been *falling*. All that time, I had been flying. I was flying down because I was looking down. To fly up, I only needed to look up.

When I returned to the United States, I swallowed my pride and joined a real estate office, taking a job as a managing broker. On my own time, I flipped small properties, scaling up as my resources allowed, with my son, Michael, helping me.

Soon I left the real estate office to flip houses full-time. We opened a general construction company because the villages wanted permits pulled by a licensed and bonded general contractor. In time, I began serving others by managing their projects as well. I started to see the need for talented inspectors with strong communication skills. *City Home* Inspectors was born.

A NEW PERSPECTIVE

When the pandemic struck, it had nothing on us. My oldest son and daughter joined me and Michael in my business. Business boomed as we scaled up both our general construction and home inspection businesses. Eventually, we decided to focus on home inspection exclusively because it brought us together and we enjoyed it.

It's a blessing helping homebuyers achieve the American dream. It's also a blessing to run a successful business with my children. Has it always been easy? Of course not, but it was worth it. Thanks to lessons from my parents and the passion I discovered when I was young, I was able to recognize opportunity and find role models, like my aunt, Lydia Rodriguez-Saldana; my sister, Sabrina Rodriguez; and my associates, Maggie Antillon-Mathews and Carmen Chucrala, who inspired me along the way.

The falling dream is gone, but real estate has taught me to keep my head up and never give up.

MY REAL ESTATE INSPIRATION

There are many reasons why someone should choose a career in real estate. If you understand that hard work pays off, the earning potential is unlimited. If you prefer a work schedule with variety, you will appreciate the flexibility and freedom the industry offers. If you are passionate about serving others, you will have the ability to make a difference in the lives of others. The benefits of a career in real estate are truly endless, as there is a wide variety of career paths one can choose from or transition into as I have proven in this short version of my story. I started as a managing broker, transitioned to a general contractor, and then became a home inspector while flipping and building properties for myself and others.

The most fascinating part of my journey is the numerous people I have met and all that I've learned. Real estate is very important because for many, it is their greatest source of wealth and savings. Real estate investments provide housing and create jobs and spaces for retail, office, and manufacturing operations. Real estate is essential and here to stay.

If you are interested in a career in real estate, surround yourselves with successful people from the industry. You will be amazed at the people in real estate who are more passionate about their jobs, in my opinion, than professionals in any other industry. We are our own bosses creating our own successes, and you can, too!

BIOGRAPHY

Baxtie Rodriguez is a serial entrepreneurial real estate professional with more than twenty-one years of experience as a managing broker. She has guided and mentored hundreds of agents and has taken home flippers, homeowners, and other home inspectors under her wing, providing invaluable lessons through her former consulting business, Bax Development Group.

As the sole owner of Bax Properties, Inc., she managed multiple real estate franchises, encompassing more than sixty-five agents simultaneously. Baxtie also is the owner of City Home Inspectors, which services homes in both the Chicagoland and Sarasota, Florida, areas, and owns and operates an online referral-based brokerage. Baxtie loves to teach and provides professional development courses to aspiring home inspectors and real estate professionals in both Illinois and Florida.

She is also a strong believer in the value of community and maintains membership in The Oak Park Area Association of Realtors®, Illinois Association of Realtors®, the National Association of Realtors®, the National Association of Hispanic Real Estate Professionals®, the American Society of Home Inspectors, the International Association of Certified Home Inspectors (InterNACHI®), and the Illinois Association of Home Inspectors.

Baxtie is proud to work daily alongside her three children who have joined her in her business ventures.

Baxtie Rodriguez
Baxie.rodriguez@yahoo.com
www.baxtie.com

REAL ESTATE WITH HEART

ROSY BELTRAN

"Run your own race and be yourself."

Who is Rosy Beltran? Well, I can say I'm a successful and fulfilled Latina for many reasons. I've done well in my career, but recently I also became a mother to twin baby girls. They have shown me so much in so little time, and being their mother is what I'm most proud of thus far in my life. For them, I want to thrive and be the best version of myself more than ever before.

My journey hasn't been easy. I come from very humble beginnings. I was born in Mexico, raised by my grandmother for the first few years of my life, and then came to the United States at the age of five to be with my parents. I grew up knowing my parents worked very hard to make ends meet. I would barely see them! My father was a cook at a restaurant so he worked long hours. By the time he came home, I'd be sleeping. My mother worked the second shift.

We lived in a small apartment, always with extra family members to help with the living expenses. At seven years old, I remember always having old or used furniture and already wondering if we would ever have a nice house with nice furniture. My parents worked so hard they certainly deserved it!

AN EARLY CALLING

I also knew at an early age that I wanted more out of life. I wanted to make my parents proud and also make something of myself. So, I set out with that goal in mind, and wow, what a journey it has been!

For some agents, the passion for real estate starts at an early age. It was the same with me. I fell in love with real estate before I could even get licensed. I was always interested in it. As a teenager, I would drive around different neighborhoods and look at all the different properties. I knew real estate was what I wanted to do.

Real estate was always an interest of mine, but I couldn't get licensed until I was twenty-one. So, I worked a full-time job at a cell phone store in a small plaza in the Belmont Cragin area of Chicago. Coincidentally, it's an area where I've now sold many homes. At the time, I also was attending college full time studying business administration. I was getting ready to graduate with my bachelor's degree when I decided to take my first real estate class. I was now old enough to become licensed and begin my dream career. I graduated college and obtained my real estate license all in the same year.

I remember my parents encouraging me to just look for a regular corporate, nine-to-five job. Wasn't that the reason I went to college and got a degree? But I knew deep down that I was born to be an entrepreneur and have my own business through real estate. It was then when I realized I had to be my own cheerleader and believe in myself.

RISE AND FALL

I'll never forget those early years. I got licensed in November 2005, not even knowing where to begin. I started my real estate journey at Century 21 Salamanca in the Bucktown neighborhood of Chicago. It also was where I took my real estate class. It was a super fun, lively, Latin-owned office, with many successful Latin agents. They would have monthly meetings that were like parties, where they would give awards to the top producers. There was music and food and everyone had fun.

This was all very motivational for me because, at that time, I was one of their youngest agents. I was humble and unaccustomed to making big amounts of money. When I had my first closing, I couldn't believe it. Here I was, twenty-one years old, making a $10,000 commission check from my $400,000 cash sale, while doing what I always wanted to do. This was my dream job! Six months into my real estate career, I made a decision to switch brokerage firms and joined RE/MAX City in May of 2006, where I grew as an agent. But things were going to change.

We were just a few years away from the big market crash of 2008. Not realizing what was coming, I just had purchased my first multi-unit property and luxury dream truck at the age of twenty-three. Then suddenly, not only was I young and inexperienced, but the market was in shambles. I had lost everything, including my income. I gave up my luxury car and can still remember borrowing money from friends and family that year, just to keep on my cell phone and to be able to serve clients. I remember going door to door, cold calling, and getting a lot of noes from people while out looking for new business. You name it, and I went through it.

I learned then how important it is to seize opportunities when they arise and to build strong business relationships with good referral partners. I had been so young and new to real estate when the crisis hit that my only choice was to muster what resilience I had within me.

I did feel like I had failed when I was forced to take a few steps back. I had to move back home with my parents, downgrade my car, and regroup to evolve with the current market. I prayed a lot, and didn't know what was going to happen. I only knew that quitting at that time wasn't an option. This was what I was born to do and I wasn't going to let anything get in the way.

Those difficult times humbled us all very quickly. I remember seeing many of my colleagues—top agents I admired—also lose everything during this crash, including properties, luxury cars, etc. Some left the business altogether. But I was determined to overcome those rocky times. I don't even remember how I managed to stay afloat. I just knew I had to start all over again and build myself up back from nothing. It wasn't easy but I thank

God for helping me get through those tough times and always put good people in my path.

For example, I remember getting a phone call one day from a female lender, who owned a couple of mortgage offices. I had never met her before, but her main office was nearby. She found me in a real estate magazine, *Su Casa Su Guia*, we both advertised in at the time. When we met, I quickly learned how successful she was. We also clicked with each other immediately.

"I want us to work together," she said. This woman, Marcy Guzman, became a big mentor for me and ended up giving me tremendous opportunities. She was a successful mortgage broker who was also a strong, successful Latina who helped me through a hard time in the industry. She also was the person to push me to invest in real estate, and helped me to buy my first multi-unit at the age of twenty-three. Thank you, Marcy Guzman, for making a difference in my life! Winning and losing isn't everything. Sometimes the journey is just as important as the outcome.

As the years passed, I had similar experiences throughout my career. I connected with incredible people which yielded great business relationships with lenders and other real estate professionals. The rest was history.

CHANGING TIMES

Times have definitely changed from 2005, and the way we do business has changed, too. With all the resources we have today to easily reach people, especially through the power of social media, we are able to help more clients than ever before.

We can't deny that social media has changed our business for good. It's an important tool for any real estate professional and I have gotten many clients off of my social media platforms. My only advice is to not lose a sense of reality, be yourself, be relatable, and be human. Everyone knows what we do for a living, so simply showcase the reality of it all. When people can relate to you and like you, the business will follow.

Even in this digital age, I'm still "old school" and grateful to have experienced real estate before we were connecting online. I think back on those times and smile; I'm glad I never gave up on myself, or on my dream. It's a beautiful thing when a career and a passion come together.

When I speak to young and up-and-coming real estate agents, I always tell them to run your own race and to be yourself. I think it took me longer to grow and understand many aspects of the business because I was scared to ask for help. I wanted to have control over it all on my own, and that's very difficult. We will never know everything, and that's okay. What has worked for another agent might not work for you. That's why I always tell people to be yourself, find your niche, and run with it. No one is you and that is your power!

Also, sometimes people look at this business from the outside in and only see the success. But when you are starting, it is not going to be easy. It is like any new business; you will have to build it from the ground up and it will take time. Be persistent. Giving up should not be an option. When you need help, ask for it. Surround yourself with people who inspire and motivate you. Find a mentor you can learn from. Learn to evolve when it's necessary, become resourceful, and always bring value to the table.

Even though working in real estate is financially rewarding, the true reward is the feeling I get from helping people, especially those who have come a long way to make homeownership a reality. Because I came from modest beginnings myself, I can relate to the struggles people face when buying a house, and the uncertainty they have about whether they can make a purchase that large. I enjoy helping families who at one time might have thought that the idea of owning a home was simply an impossible dream. I remember my parents struggling when I was a child, so it's a very rewarding feeling to help families build wealth and achieve the goal of owning a home through real estate.

I'm successful because I conduct my business with heart. I truly care about my client's best interest and that they are truly content with their entire experience with me. If my clients aren't happy, neither am I. I genuinely care and I know my clients know it because the majority of my business is from referrals.

My success in the industry has not gone unnoticed. I have consecutively been named a Top Producer by the Chicago Association of Realtors®, I have been featured in Top Agent Magazine and I have the opportunity to be part of this amazing book. I'm a proud Latina and it is an honor to be part of this project with other successful and inspiring Latinas, who are paving the way for the next generation.

MY REAL ESTATE INSPIRATION

If you are thinking of becoming a real estate agent you can look into classes at Chicago Association of Realtors® for upcoming classes. You'll never know how great you can be at something until you do it!

I also would like to share with you some good reads that have helped me in my business:

- *Rich Dad, Poor Dad* by Robert Kiyosaki
- *The Four Agreements* by Don Michael Ruiz
- *You are a Badass* by Jen Sincero

BIOGRAPHY

Rosy Beltran, a real estate professional since 2005, is a real estate broker at RE/MAX Properties, serving the Chicagoland area. Rosy takes pride in always looking out for the best interest of her clients. She has a strong track record of success because she focuses on building long-term relationships with everyone.

For Rosy, the only way to have a successful real estate transaction is to look at the clients' big picture. She takes everything into consideration and is always thinking about the long-term implications of each investment. Her clients are her extended family, for without them, her career would not be possible.

Rosy's mission is to continue helping as many families as possible achieve the American dream of home ownership. She also seeks to practice what she preaches by continuing to grow her own real estate investment portfolio alongside her life partner, Arturo Vargas. Rosy is also the proud mother of twin baby girls, Gianna and Giselle. She enjoys traveling at least once a year and is excited to continue doing this with her daughters. She's also a self-proclaimed foodie who loves trying out new restaurants, and loves everything to do with fashion.

Rosy Beltran
rbeltran@remax.net
Instagram: @rosybeltranrealtor

FOLLOWING MY ENTREPRENEURIAL SOUL

JOHANNA DIAZ

"I didn't stop. I never quit. I kept going."

I was born in 1983 in a small city called Pereira, Colombia, in the coffee axis region. It's covered with beautiful mountains and beautiful people. My father had a well-known steakhouse and my mom owned a shop that sold electronics downtown. I truly believe I inherited my entrepreneurial passion from them.

Our whole family is very close on both sides. Every weekend we gathered at my *tio's* farm and just spent time with each other. I was raised with many cousins and our lives were very happy.

Hustle has been a part of my life since I was a little girl. I remember asking my father to give me money to buy candies and chips to sell at my school when I was eight years old. The first day, I sold it all and came back to my dad. I told him I made lots of money and I was so happy. He quickly explained to me that all that money wasn't mine; I needed to pay him back, and with the money left over, I was to buy more product to continue sustaining my business. That was the very first time I got introduced to the words, "capital" and "debt," and I felt poor for a bit until the business picked up. I grew that little business so well that girls from other classrooms would come to buy from me. Then I was on the nun's radar.

One time when she caught me selling goodies, she took them from me, wrote a note to take to my father, and that was the end of my little hustle. Well, at least for a while. My brother was very good at drawing and painting, so I told him to start a business with me since I had clientele. Around Christmas time, we sold tons of Christmas cards and other seasonal stickers.

OPPORTUNITY IN THE USA

In 1999, my dad decided to move to the United States because of the lack of opportunities in Colombia. His business was not running the way he wanted, and we were accumulating debt, so he moved to New Jersey with my brother. My mom and I stayed in Colombia. It was very hard to be separated; I can't even imagine what families go through when they are not together.

Finally, after nine long months of being separated, my mom and I joined them in Chicago. Luckily, my father had a business visa so we were all able to immigrate legally and make a future in the United States. When my dad picked us up from the airport, we were so happy to be together, but it was terribly cold. I felt it down to my bones, and I was suddenly depressed. I would never forget the song that was playing on the radio at the time. It was called "Blue," and perfectly described my feelings.

When we got home, we had two mattresses on the floor, my parent's bedroom set, food in the fridge, and lots of love. To be honest, that's all we needed! We just wanted to be together. Still, immigrating wasn't easy! I arrived in the country without knowing the language and was then thrown into a high school where I didn't look like everyone else.

At the time, my dad was working at a senior retirement place. The residents were wealthy, and our job was to help them move in and out. My dad worked there every day and my mom, brother, and I joined him on the weekends to help. Every time a resident passed away, their children would ask us to take their belongings and sell them or keep them ourselves. Yes, that is how we furnished our home. We would take everything else that was left over and wake up at four o'clock in the morning that Sunday to take it to the flea market and sell it for a profit.

Years later, my dad opened a piggy bank business. We would sell handmade piggy banks to supermarkets and dollar stores. After that he went on to import flower vases from Colombia to sell to flower shops. Later, we distributed jeans and body shapers all over the Chicago area. I was helping the whole time while earning my business degree from a community college. I continued working part-time with my father as I went on to Robert Morris University and then Keller Graduate School of Management.

THE CONVERSATION

After college, my plans were to find a high-paying job, contribute towards my 401(k) and Social Security, and then retire at sixty-two and be happy. The more I worked towards that, the emptier I felt. I'm not sure what it was, but I think my entrepreneur soul was telling me I had a better chance of making it on my own with a good idea and lots of strategy.

When I was in my sixth year at Bank of America, I had a pivotal conversation that sent me in that direction. I was the manager there, overseeing twelve employees in the biggest branch in the district. We were very successful, but I was absolutely drained.

Just months earlier, I had been introduced to credit repair when my husband and I wanted to purchase our first property. He is a former Marine who served in Iraq. When he returned home, his credit was shattered, so we worked to recover it. Once we were successful, I had an idea to share the knowledge and strategies we had learned with others. I started helping people fix their credit, and I loved it. I felt purposeful and fulfilled every time someone ended up buying a home after fixing their credit.

Meanwhile, my husband had found a mentor who was a successful millionaire business owner that God put in our path to ground us and guide us. I remember an evening with him at Gibson's Steakhouse as we talked through two opportunities I had: joining the wealth management team at Bank of America or starting my own credit repair business to specifically service the Hispanic community.

"Which one are you leaning toward?" he asked.

"Obviously wealth management," I replied, going on to explain why it was such a great position and how I would be dealing with wealthy people and their finances. He listened patiently and what he said next was my turning point.

"Johanna, can I tell you something but promise me you are not going to take it the wrong way and you are really going to listen to my words?"

"Tiralo," I replied, which means "throw it" in Spanish.

"Johanna, you are a woman, you are young, you are Latina, and you are broke," he said. "Please tell me what rich person is going to trust you with their finances? YES! You will make it and I have no doubts you will, but you will have so many struggles and challenges you may get discouraged. Now, let's talk about this business idea of yours, credit repair with a focus on the Hispanic market. Again, you are a woman, you are young, you are Hispanic, and you are broke. Everyone will love you and trust you with their lives, and you will be successful without any hiccups."

I could have let my feelings get the best of me, but instead I chose to listen to what someone else was saying to me that others wouldn't for fear it was not politically correct. I listened, appreciated what he said, and took it into consideration.

Then one day I was so overwhelmed and exhausted when I got home from work that I went to my husband, Oscar, and cried my eyes out, telling him that I was done with the bank job and that I wanted to work on my credit repair business.

"Do you think I don't know you are going to make this work? Send that resignation letter immediately and go for it!" he said.

When I called my brother to tell him, he asked if I needed help painting my new office! He came with my nephews and we painted my little back room green and decorated it. There, I toiled from 7 a.m. to 11 p.m., every day. I didn't stop. I never quit. I kept going.

THINKING BIGGER

By October 2015, I told Oscar to join me and that was difficult for us. I thought I was his boss at work and at home, and that didn't sit well with him. We fought constantly, but he stayed with me until I was able to hire my first administrative assistant so he could leave!

In 2022, Credit Rx has grown to twelve employees. It also has a Spanish call center in Puerto Rico, an English call center in the Philippines, and a sales department in Chicago, Illinois. We service the entire United States and have created numerous relationships with real estate professionals and lenders throughout the years. Oscar went on to become a successful real estate agent with a team of two beautiful and hardworking ladies who are closing all his deals.

Many people ask me where I get my passion for real estate and my answer is very simple—my husband! Oscar and I met in 2011, fell deeply in love, and married six months later. Fast huh? As he says, "When you know, you know!"

Remember that millionaire friend I talked about? Well, he used to get haircuts from my husband, and became my husband's mentor. Every week our friend would show us properties for sale and talk about how to create wealth through rents and positive cashflow. He took the time to teach my husband, who was raised in poverty and had little financial knowledge, how to become a beast at real estate investing.

I clearly remember the day my husband wanted to purchase a property and I told him, "Babe! I want a big house with lots of space." He quickly knocked me out of my little bubble.

"No ma'am. We are getting a building!"

We bought our first investment property in 2014. It was a massive three-unit on the north side of Chicago, which opened doors to financial security and allowed us to sustain our little business while we grew it. My husband's family is from Puerto Rico, and he has great love for the island. He always wanted to make a living there, so we started working towards that by finally purchasing our first Airbnb in Aguadilla. After that, we continued to increase our investment portfolio on the island and then rented out twelve properties for short and long-term rentals. Due to our investment experience in the Puerto Rico and the Airbnb market, we started a consulting company to bring in more investors and teach them how to become profitable through the purchase of second homes and investment properties.

My ultimate goal is to sustain myself through passive income, so I can pursue full-time missionary work. I began to know Christ Jesus in 2011, and from that point on, my life took a big turn for the better. Knowing him is all I need, so I work hard through his grace so that one day I can be used to financially bless others. I don't do any of this through my own strength, I do so through God who strengthens me. I hope to serve him for the rest of my days.

MY REAL ESTATE INSPIRATION

In my humble opinion, real estate is what keeps the world

turning! I think that responsibly owning a piece of land that eventually will have equity is, and always will be, the safest and most secure way to build wealth. Being a real estate owner and living around others who own their real estate will make your community stronger, more valuable, and a delight to live in. For Latinas, the idea of owning several properties and creating wealth through real estate is unusual. But if this Colombian immigrant, who came with nothing can end up owning 12 properties, so can you!

Ask yourself these questions. Was I taught about real estate before? Who am I spending time with? Do they bring value to my life and my future finances? Or am I wasting my best years in temporary pleasures? How many "negative Nancys" do I have in my life? How do I change that? If you are interested in real estate, one of the best things you can do for yourself is to surround yourself with like-minded people, who are successful at what YOU are trying to accomplish!

Remember to never quit, and always keep going! You have NOTHING to lose!

BIOGRAPHY

Johanna Diaz is a real estate investor and the founder of Credit Rx. She hails from Pereira, Colombia, and was raised by entrepreneurial parents before they moved to the United States when she was a teen. Throughout her life, Johanna has been driven by her entrepreneurial spirit and belief in education. She earned a master's degree in sales and marketing from the Keller Graduate School of Management and worked as a branch manager at Bank of America, managing the largest and most successful branch in her district.

In 2011, Johanna met an amazing Marine veteran, Oscar Diaz, and they were married six months later. Inspired by their personal home-buying experiences and the need to repair their credit, Johanna founded Credit Rx. The company concentrates on the Hispanic market and helps clientele find financial freedom and opportunity with solutions to their credit problems. Credit Rx serves clients throughout the United States and Puerto Rico.

In 2022, Johanna earned her real estate license in Puerto Rico and is working with investors for the purchase of properties to be converted into vacation rentals there. She enjoys the challenge of real estate and looks forward to the future.

Johanna Diaz
johanna@credit-rx.com
Facebook: @creditrx2015

A PLACE TO CALL HOME

MAGALY "MAGGIE" MARTINEZ

"My career journey, just like my childhood, was full of moves and new beginnings."

One of the most vivid childhood memories I have is contemplating my limits at the age of five.

I was sitting on a huge rock, so big that it seemed impossible to move. I looked down at my feet, which were covered with dirt because I loved running around without shoes. I recall the feeling of being ordinary, and the urge to look up and beyond, hoping to see a glimpse of my future. Instead, all I saw was an endless panoramic view of *los cerros* (the hills). They, too, seemed so permanently fixed.

Even though the view was extraordinary and the serenity brought my heart closer to my Creator, I didn't want it. I felt stuck in the middle of the immensity, and all I could do was wonder what else was out there for me.

HOPING TO BELONG

For the first six years of my life, I lived in Jose Maria Morelos or Chinacates, a large village located in Durango, Mexico. My mother and I lived in my grandparent's home. It was a beautiful pueblo-style house with three *corrales* (pens) and a huge patio in the middle of the structure. It was a stunning home, but it felt lonely after my *abuelos* (grandparents) relocated to Chicago, Illinois. They wanted to live closer to most of their children who, one by one had migrated to the United States to pursue a better life, or at least one with better infrastructure and accommodations. For pueblo folks, having access to clean water, a warm shower, and a stove to cook a meal on was worth the sacrifice of leaving everything behind. As a result, most of my extended family was in the United States except for my mom, two of her sisters, their families, and me.

My mom had me at the age of twenty and was a single parent. At the time she conceived, she had no intention of having my biological father involved in my life. I think she was concerned that if he stuck around, she would be pressured by her family and society to commit to him. It was easier for her to take responsibility for raising me on her own. Eventually, I met my father and understood her decision. He is a good person, but in his younger years he was a ladies' man who did not help raise his children.

When I was four years old, my mother married, and from that marriage, she conceived four amazing children who have been blessings in my life. I have three beautiful, smart, and kind sisters. They have repeatedly shown up for me in selfless ways throughout the years. My youngest sibling is my little brother, who through his personal struggles has given me the courage to love and accept myself.

My mom and stepdad moved around quite a bit when I was young as we tried to find a place to called *home*. At first, we temporarily moved into my mother's childhood home. Two years later and with their first child on the way, my stepdad became desperate to have our family claim our independence and, most importantly, to reclaim his manhood. Who wants to live at their in-law's house for that long?

My stepdad was a U.S. citizen and my mother and I were fortunate enough to have our residency, thanks to Ronald Reagan's 1986 amnesty and my Tia Tencha, who submitted the petition for us. She changed the course my life with this act of kindness. It seemed like nothing stood between us and a new life in the states until my sister, Indira, decided to enter this world, prematurely, and on the wrong side of the border!

We stayed and embraced our pueblo life long enough for me to enjoy having a baby sister and teach her how to walk. Soon, though, the unhappiness and the frustration of day-to-day living pushed my mom to leave her baby behind with my aunt in Durango, with the intention to visit Indira every month or two until she received her green card and could meet us in Chicago.

It was a winter night in 1999 when we arrived in the Windy City. I looked outside the window of the 1970 Grand Marquis my stepdad had borrowed from a friend to get us around while we settled. I read the street signs until we pulled up in front of a beautiful, brown brick three-flat. I could not believe it was going to be my new home. I was so excited! I still remember meeting all of my aunts and cousins and feeling full of love and support. However, I also felt guilty when I noticed how sad my mom was. A day did not pass when I didn't see her cry because she missed my sister.

As we settled in and both my parents started working, my mother was increasingly absent. She always seemed worried and overwhelmed, especially when my stepdad was around. She was constantly looking to appease him. It was so irritating that I began resenting him because his presence made me feel small and invisible. Nevertheless, I understood because I was always very good at justifying other people's actions, and I was raised to be polite and respectful towards my elders. I couldn't complain because, hey, it could have been me that got left behind in Mexico.

Nothing felt better than to be close to my *abuelos* (grandparents) again. *My Abuela Leonor* made everything OK, especially when I was missing my mom and barely saw her because she was working the graveyard shift. *Abuela Leonor* was always proud of me and reminded me every day of how special I was. I remember the warmth of her hands when she would grab my face to kiss my forehead and tell me that I was *una mujer chingona* (a cool woman) who would change lives. Those words of affirmation pushed me through many obstacles in my life.

Between my grandparent's love, the endless summer days playing tag with my cousins, and playing in the water whenever one of the older kids would open the sidewalk fire hydrant, I can say that those days in Chicago were the happiest times in my childhood.

MOVING ON

Unfortunately, we didn't spend very long in Chicago. We moved a couple times before my family permanently settled once again in Nuevo Ideal, Durango, Mexico, not far from our hometown. I resented the move because I felt that instead of getting closer to opportunities, I was drifting away from them. In a small town, there were few choices, and I did not want to be a burden to my mother. She had her hands full and spent most of her days running after my four siblings, making sure they were dressed, fed, and well cared for. It was clear to me that if I wanted more than what my parents were able to offer, I had to create my own path. So, to no one's surprise, I moved back to Chicago right after graduating high school.

Like many people, my past self had a loud voice in my future decisions. It was a voice that at times reminded me of how brave and empowered I was. At other times, it left me feeling empty with a low sense of belonging. My twenties were a rollercoaster, both emotionally and financially, but I had enough fire in me to work multiple jobs. I was able to get through college, live independently, and get by comfortably. I became a mother for the first time at the age of twenty-three and experienced all the trials and sacrifices that come with motherhood. For me, that included a failed, premature marriage.

During that time, I learned many lessons, which allowed me to appreciate my husband when I finally met him. He came into my life with so much love and respect that our relationship allowed me to heal, and most importantly, create our home and family.

It is interesting that all the twist and turns in my life led me to where I am today. My career journey, just like my childhood, was full of moves and new beginnings. God blessed me with a versatile personality and the desire to help others, so I was always naturally drawn to sales. It made sense that I would eventually end up there.

A NEW LIFE IN REAL ESTATE

When I was twenty-eight years old, I was working in corporate America for one of the largest financial companies in my area. I was burnt out, discouraged, and unmotivated. Climbing the corporate ladder as a woman is challenging. Although it's not impossible, I just lacked the stamina to push through all the obstacles created by unconscious (and many times, conscious) gender biases. I also began to doubt the value of the products and services I was presenting to my community. So, I began to look beyond corporate banking for something new.

Right after giving birth to my son, Mateo, in 2014, I took a leap of faith and joined the real estate industry as a licensed real estate professional. It was a move that led me to connect with my good friend, Maggie Antillon. Although I was still searching for my place in real estate, being a real estate professional gave me the lens to view what the mortgage world could offer my forever thrill-seeking heart. I liked what I saw and got my mortgage license at the end of 2018.

My goal as a mortgage loan officer is to make a difference in my community. I explored every possibility for deserving families that want to qualify for a loan. I made the career jump because I saw the need for true mortgage professionals, and I knew that my skills, heart, and hustle could benefit the mortgage field. To be successful in the mortgage industry, a loan officer needs transparency, accountability, love for people, and the passion to help them. And I have that passion.

It's lovely to see how every single family that I've helped has their own story. I've helped young families with the desire to embrace their love; young immigrants battling social differences and just trying to find their place here; blended families excited for a new beginning; multi-generational families trying to work together to live more comfortably; parents helping their children open their wings and leave the nest; and, of course, fellow entrepreneurs building their legacy and trying to change the narrative for our Latino people. When I hear their stories, I can relate to them. Because at one point, all I wanted, too, was a place to call home.

In 2021, my third full year in the mortgage industry, many congratulated me on my overnight success. I'm constantly told that very few can accomplish what I have built in such a short time. The reality is that, day in and day out, the workload is balanced by the commitment I make to those who choose to do business with me and trust that I will show up at my best to help them. The results are just the byproduct of my work ethic.

The reason I share all the details of my personal story is to assure you that if a little girl sitting on a rock, pondering life, was able to find her calling in real estate, so can you. The beautiful thing about this industry is that anyone can play. The access to opportunities is endless. There will always be a fountain of wealth to drink from. Whether you are buying, selling, or funding real estate, you can find your gold ticket navigating the sea of possibilities—the one that I recently set sail upon.

Although my *abuela* is no longer with me, I'm sure she would be proud of me because my life has fulfilled her prophecy. I **do** help people, I **do** change their lives, and I think that's what makes me **chingona** *(a bad-ass woman)!*

MY REAL ESTATE INSPIRATION

I'm a big believer that your abilities are not fixed, but instead, something that can be developed. However, you must think big. You must want to do good for others, you must be intentional about your goals and direction, and you must surround yourself with the best! So, as you are getting ready to embark on your real estate career, keep in mind that you need to go into your journey willing to be a student and ready to work and give it your all. The more focus and dedication you have in the beginning, the faster you will propel your business forward.

It is also equally important that you MUST protect your entrepreneurial vision. Remember, people who lack the clarity, courage, or determination to follow their own dreams will often find a way to discourage yours. Love your TRUTH and don't EVER stop! and if you are successful, it's because somewhere, sometime, someone gave you a life or an idea that pushed you in the right direction. Nobody succeeds alone. Check your ego and always be grateful.

"Success is not counted by how high you have climbed but by how many people you brought with you."
-Dr. Wil Rose

BIOGRAPHY

Magaly "Maggie" Martinez is more than a mortgage adviser; she is a mortgage expert. Her financial and real estate background give her significant insight into her clients' options. Maggie has recently joined Guaranteed Rate, the third largest lender in the United States, as a branch manager. She services the Latino community through top-notch customer service, technology, and programs, and empowers other real estate professionals to grow with her.

Maggie offers honest advice on loans for first-time home buying experiences, to purchasing investment properties, to refinancing residential mortgages. Her knowledge and youthful demeanor are an asset to her clients. She is a wife and a mother of two young children and can relate to what buying a home means not only for an individual, but for the entire family. Maggie truly loves to make the experience of home buying a pleasant one.

Maggie has dedicated her entire business to providing outstanding customer support with caring and sound advice and full transparency. Her main goal is to leverage all her resources to continue to close the gap in Hispanic homeownership, all while paving the future for Latinos to have easier access to the generational wealth that can be built through real estate.

Magaly "Maggie" Martinez
Maggie.martinez@rate.com
630-460-0688

FROM FALLEN EMPIRE TO FAMILY LEGACY

CARMEN CHUCRALA

"If I had not gone through this, I would not be the person I am today."

Let me start by saying that being an entrepreneur is difficult, but being a Latina entrepreneur in the real estate world is even harder, especially when you are five-feet tall like me.

I first entered real estate when I was sixteen years old. I was born in Palmira, Colombia, a town outside of Cali, to teenage parents. I lived in Colombia until I was four years old, before we moved to Chicago. Since my mom was sixteen and my father was eighteen, my grandmother made my mother leave school and work to support me. My father left us on the day of my eighth-grade graduation. My mother worked long hours to give me everything I needed, and she always encouraged me to fulfill my dreams.

In the eighth grade, I was only one of two students accepted into Lane Tech College Prep High School, a very competitive magnet school in Chicago. I didn't want to attend, but my mom didn't give me an option.

I remember needing money for lunch but feeling bad about asking my mom for it because we were barely making ends meet. Then one day after school, I saw a flyer for a job at the Century 21 Salamanca real estate office. I applied to work there after school. Mr. Salamanca told me the job could change my life and I might even fall in love. I remember laughing and thinking *I'm going away to college, and I am too young to fall in love. Still, I got the job and real estate became part of my life.*

A CHANGE IN PLANS

I became the receptionist, then the administrative assistant. Then a real estate school opened and I started helping with the school. I even tutored the real estate students. One student and I started dating. Five years later, he became the father of my children. Mr. Salamanca was right!

When the real estate instructor decided to open her own school, I followed her. When I turned twenty-one, she handed me a transcript and said I knew all the material, I had put in the hours, I deserved to get my license, and I should take the test. I told her I was planning to go to college for finance, move to New York, work on Wall Street, and then eventually move to Europe to use my six years of French! Still, she convinced me to sit for the exam and I passed. I was so happy. I didn't realize my teacher had given me a transcript to obtain a broker's license, which is the equivalent of a managing broker's license now!

I returned to Century 21 Salamanca with my license and sold a few homes. Then, when I was about to graduate from DePaul University with a degree in finance and marketing, my mom gave me $3,000 to go to Europe where I could use my French! I was genuinely touched that she had managed to save so much money for me.

I didn't go to Europe. Instead, I asked a co-worker if he wanted to partner up and buy a two-flat, using a Federal Housing Administration (FHA) loan. I only had the $3,000 and my income, but he agreed, even though neither one of us knew what we were doing. When we ran out of money, we pawned our cars, getting "cash for title." It was sad since my mom had refinanced her house to pay off that car so I wouldn't have any debt.

There was no YouTube back in 2002, so we learned how to install flooring from a book. We would work our full-time jobs during the day and work on the units at night. We ordered pizza and ate on the floor as we finished our work. Once our renovation was complete, we refinanced the two-flat, made $70.000 each and rented the units, making $1,200 a month profit. We were hooked.

Life was good. I was enjoying myself working and spending time with my family. I quit my full-time job and went into real estate for the financial freedom and independence. The business was prospering at an alarming rate. After I saw my first commission check, I started my own brokerage.

As an immigrant from Colombia and the first-generation in

the United States to go to college, I had a multi-million-dollar business at just twenty-seven years old. Someone once told me that I could never be a millionaire because I had a green card. I would tell people it didn't matter. I would build an empire before I turned thirty!

CRASH AND CARRY

The real estate market was red hot. I was running a business where I was my own boss, and I was helping many people obtain the dream of homeownership. I was investing in my own properties, and making unbelievable money for someone in her twenties. Then it happened. The real estate crash of 2008. The housing bubble burst and it was like something right out of a movie. My empire was falling.

Thoughts filled my head. My business. My age. A net worth of $3.2 million. I tried to stay afloat, because my parents taught me that we were defined by the Social Security number we had been given to get credit. I couldn't be defined by a number. I had used up all my savings to pay the mortgages and maintain my office. Now, tenants had stopped paying, agents stopped selling, and people were saying buying a home was the American nightmare, not the American dream. I started believing it myself. All my work and time building my empire was gone forever. I couldn't believe it. It was like a bad dream.

I stood there, watching the movers pack up the files and furniture from the business I had worked so hard to build. It felt as though a piece of my heart was being packed away and sealed up, too. I had no tears in my eyes—just a ghostly stare. During the "rise of the empire," my children's father and I had parted. I was now a single mother with two young children, who relied solely on me. I had failed not only as an owner, but as a mother. The look in their innocent eyes pierced like a knife in my heart.

"*Mami* why are those people moving your stuff?" my son asked.

What would you tell your four-year-old son?

The next few days I was numb. I had been taught that crying was a sign of weakness, so I couldn't do it. I tried everything. I called the banks and asked for some type of modification to my loans. I owned a property in the Bucktown neighborhood of Chicago with the last appraised value of $680,000 that now was valued at $150,000. No one would help, and I felt powerless. People at the bank told me to file for bankruptcy. I would not do that to my credit score.

Instead, I ended up selling my house on a short sale that I couldn't do myself because I owned it. A month later, I got a letter from the bank telling me they approved my modification, and my mortgage would reduce from $2,400 to $980! I became more and more infuriated with real estate. It was like post-traumatic stress disorder (PTSD); I couldn't even watch those fake HGTV shows. Many colleagues still suggested bankruptcy, reminding me that we are not defined by our credit score.

On December 31, 2010 (the worst year of my life), I gave in and told my attorney to file bankruptcy. It was like signing the official fall of my empire.

STRENGTH IN EDUCATION

I have always believed God has a purpose for all of us. When people ask me what I would have done differently, I always say, "Nothing." If I had experienced something else, I would not be the person I am today. I made a lot of money and gave money to help people, but I never had internal peace. It was all part of my journey to humbleness.

On January 1, 2011, I felt liberated. I told myself, *it can only go up from here*. I was done feeling sorry for myself and determined to come back stronger. A friend of mine suggested I take a course called Landmark Education. The course saved my life and rebuilt my future!

I changed my mindset and now call my $3.2-million-dollar bankruptcy a $3.2-million- dollar education. I vowed to never have any of my clients go through what I went through. Before becoming a full-time Realtor, I was an accountant and consultant. I was grateful to reenter the field when the market crashed, and continue to work in real estate part time. I started educating myself on proper investing, tax implications, and diversifying portfolios. I started passing on information to my clients as part of my service at no cost. God had me experience bankruptcy so I could protect other people from it. I changed my mindset from having a bankrupted fallen empire to being able to educate others for a legacy of generational wealth.

Fast-forward to today and you'll find I am a humble Realtor who believes in putting people first. On January 11, 2011, I started a new brokerage company called Habloft. The name was inspired by a Colombian novela about beautiful women in real estate development with a company named Habiloft. I didn't like the sound of the "i" so I adopted the name Habloft.

Habloft was never meant to be a brokerage for other agents, but people started asking to join me. I would tell them I was not set up with tools like the other brokerages, but I could offer them an education based on experience. They still signed up!

In 2013, I met the love of my life, Richard Munoz, at a networking event. He is now my husband, and along with my mother, Nancy, he's my biggest cheerleader. I kept consulting, but I wanted to pursue real estate full time, even though I was afraid I'd fail. He told me he wouldn't let that happen. On my birthday, September 5, 2016, I gave myself a gift and wrote a letter of resignation to my consulting firm. I planned to return to my passions: real estate and real estate education.

I started teaching and consulting for Midwest Real Estate Data (MRED) and Habloft started growing. Habloft means the world to me because it's a new way of doing real estate. I took my $3.2 million education and transferred it to our agents. I believe in inclusion and collaboration without competition. We don't recruit agents; our company has grown because our agents refer other agents to the company without any referral compensation. It is a company built on family and teamwork. It was what I was meant to do.

I am also a huge advocate of generational wealth. In 2020, right before COVID-19 hit, I co-founded a real estate school with my mentor from my teenage years, Sue Miranda, and my business partner, Cleo Aquino. The school reflects our philosophies and is called Successful Paths in Real Estate (SPIRE). I became a top-selling agent in the Galewood neighborhood of Chicago and I hold licenses in three other states. My legacy will be to advocate for generational wealth done right.

I tell new agents to enjoy the fruits of their labor, but always to plan for the unknown. Above all, educate Latino communities on homeownership. Don't sell a home just to sell something; make sure you educate them on protecting their assets. Also, balance your work life. It is easy to get burned out. Remember your WHY. When you put people first, the money will follow.

MY REAL ESTATE INSPIRATION

I chose real estate because I believe it is one of the very few ways to create generational wealth. It is also a pathway to financial freedom. Real estate has awarded me the opportunity to attend every one of the games that my son, Brandon, and daughter, Alessa, ever played. I take time off when I need it, without having to ask anyone but me! I also love to educate others, and real estate has allowed me to shape the new generation of real estate agents.

I am in real estate for the most important people in my life: my children, my mother, Nancy, my stepfather, Fabio, and my husband, Richard. My generation is a generation who cares for parents and our children. I am on a mission to create a legacy and generational wealth, education, and assets for future generations.

Stay informed and keep educating yourself. Sign up for organizations that align with your morals and beliefs, such as the National Association of Hispanic Real Estate Professionals. Always be a voice for our community. Know that the path in real estate can take you further than you can imagine with dedication and time. Read books and check out our real estate school, SPIRE Real Estate Education at www.SPIRERealEstateEducation.com.

BIOGRAPHY

Carmen Chucrala is founder and managing broker of Habloft, LLC, a Chicago-based brokerage focused on real estate investments and portfolio diversification. The company provides an umbrella of services for clients to protect and grow their investment dollars. With her experiences in accounting, software implementation, and real estate investments, Carmen has developed a one-stop shop business model that combines real estate and accounting services for small- to mid-sized businesses to build passive and active income.

As a co-founder of the Chicagoland Latino Investor Organization, Carmen leads a Latino-driven initiative to serve as the voice for housing providers, property owners, and investors when policies compromise the ability for families to create and preserve generational wealth. She is also the co-founder of SPIRE Real Estate Education, Inc. whose mission is to create successful paths in real estate for individuals seeking to become real estate professionals. She builds partnerships with brokerages and companies to offer pre-licensing, continuing education coursework, and onboarding and training development programs to educate, innovate and train the next generation of real estate professionals.

Carmen holds a master's degree in accounting from DeVry University's Keller Graduate School of Management and dual bachelor's degrees in marketing and finance from DePaul University.

Carmen Chucrala
chucrala1@gmail.com
(773-392-6272)

EL PAN DE VIDA (THE BREAD OF LIFE)

SALLY DELGADO, MED

"I ate Elmer's glue, crayons, and those Avon chapsticks to silence my hunger."

I remember joining the dreadful food pantry lines every month. My dad would jam my skinny, ragged body into the long line full of other hopeless families. "Quedate aqui (stay right here)," he would say, as he joined a second line. My eldest sister would take a third line so we could gather more quantities of rice, peanut butter, powered milk flakes, and my favorite—the blocked American cheese that we ate by the pound until we were constipated. As a poor family, we were trying to get through what felt like an eternity of poverty. I can recall the taste of the powered milk mixture that had to be mixed with water—it was absolutely GROSS!

I have not given it much thought until now, but I was

hungry for most of my childhood. By the time I was in second grade, I realized we were among the many families in urban Latino enclaves living below the poverty line. Every morning we had to walk thirteen blocks to get to the school breakfast bell. Sometimes we missed it and they would lock the cafeteria doors, allowing no more students to enter the building. But if you made it on time, the reward was fruitful. You got your breakfast, and if you wanted seconds, you could wait by the trash can attendant and get a second glazed donut and carton of milk.

I also acquired a taste for eating Elmer's glue, crayons, and those Avon-flavored chapsticks. I ate them all! I guess when you are curious and hungry, you'll eat anything to silence your hunger. I eventually stopped eating my glue and crayons after discovering that I enjoyed art class.

We couldn't even afford to eat at McDonald's, but the few times we did it was like all of our glory days were ahead of us. Thanks Ronald!

LEARNING AND LEADING

My dad was always on the move for a better job and quality of life since gang activity was rampant in Chicago during the 1980s. I went to six preparatory schools before I settled into the fourth grade. I even ended up in a first-grade English as Second Language (ESL) class since I was enrolled mid-year and there was no room in any other English classes. I was not aware of this until I realized that everyone around me spoke only Spanish. Like clockwork, after saying the Pledge of Allegiance and listening to the daily school announcements, the class broke out in unison singing, *"Pollito, Chicken, Gallina, Hen,"* a popular bilingual song to help Spanish-speaking children learn the English language. In that class, I made my first best friend and learned my first Spanish words before getting transferred to another school. Despite my hunger epoch, I had quite an appetite for sports and tried them all, even if I wasn't any good at them. While performing my gymnastics routine for the kids on the block, I did a full-face plant into a brick wall that left me with a busted lip, a hematoma the size of a golf ball on my forehead, and three busted teeth. I recall another time when I was about seven years old, I dialed 411 to connect me to Bela and Martha Karolyi, the famous award-winning Olympic gymnastics coaches.

"Aww, sweetie, I don't have their direct number," the operator who answered told me kindly. "Where's your mother?"

"I don't have one," I answered.

"Where's your father?" she asked.

"He's working."

"I have another local number where you can get training," she answered.

I started to tell her how we didn't have money for training and that I was certain I could make it to the next Olympic games if I could just speak with Bela.

"She said you're already a winner sweetie," she said and then hung up. I latched onto that for years.

Instead of training with the Karolyi's I joined the afterschool program and competed across Chicago Park Districts in track and field, breaking school records and snagging my spot at the top of the podium dozens of times. Naturally, I competed in high school in both track and field and cross country, earning distinctions as varsity team captain. I earned second place in state competition and my nomination as a torch runner for the 1996 Summer Olympics. It was the one thing I was good at and loved to do. Through athletic competition, I developed a deeper understanding of sportsmanship, discipline, failure, and leadership skills early on that would later serve as the glue to hold me together.

THE DELGADO FACTOR

After high school, my family decided to move to Puerto Rico, and I opted to stay in Chicago and figure things out on my own. I was nineteen. Eventually, I became homeless and found myself sleeping in my 1985 Volvo sedan more times than I would like to admit, dreaming and wishing for better circumstances.

At the age of twenty-three, I became a mother to my only son, Elijah, and by twenty-four years old, I was a single parent. I dragged my son to campus and work when I did not have anyone to care for him. And for the second time in my life, I would find myself right back in the welfare line waiting to meet the social worker. Most nights I just cried myself to sleep during what were the most difficult years, raising Elijah alone.

I made a promise to myself that after finishing my undergraduate program, I would suspend all government services. The week before commencement, I called my social worker to inform her that I was graduating and to cancel all services under my name. She told me that it would be difficult to reinstate services, but I told her she would never see me again. And they didn't!

Even in my darkness, I managed to make the dean's list each semester, for the next seven years of my degree programs. Ultimately, I earned an associate's degree and a bachelor's degree in liberal arts, then went on to earn a master's degree in education. Soon after my graduate program, I landed a role at a high school where I provided clinical mental health services for students, followed by my appointment at a community college where I immersed myself into the college student experience and held several roles.

OPULENCE AND ABUNDANCE

I stumbled into the real estate business by happenstance after meeting Eduardo (Eddie) Garcia, chief executive officer (CEO) and founder of Realty of Chicago. I was interested in having his organization support our college initiatives at the time. The decision did not come easy as I had my own professional goals mapped out, or so I thought. During the beginning of the pandemic, I had received the news that I was accepted into the doctoral program at National Louis University (NLU) for their Higher Education Leadership program. During this time, I also received two other job offers in Arizona and Florida and had started to rethink my plans.

After meeting with Eddie, it was clear that if I did not take the opportunity with his firm, I might later regret it. I always have been a very intuitive person and felt like entering real estate could be a way to fuse many aspects of my education and training and embrace a challenge to do something completely different. Before long, I joined the Realty of Chicago (ROC) team.

Soon after my formal announcement, I began receiving emails, messages, and phone calls from associates in various industries who wanted to hire me, and even others who regretted not asking me sooner. Taking the risk to join the team and asserting myself there made all the difference and convinced me that my decision to join was the right one.

Looking back, I believe that my experiences molded my character and drove me forward to succeed. I feel blessed and have a surplus of abundance in my life that I never would have had without being confident in my abilities. To utilize your superpower is to change your mindset and outlook from having nothing to envisioning more. Then persist until you get it.

FAILURE BREEDS SUCCESS

There is no magic to success. You need to put in the work, be prepared to make mistakes and lose some sleep from time to time. Before my success today, I experienced failure. I failed the entry exam for the Air Force, I failed the National Teachers Exam (NTE), and failed to meet the minimum SAT score to earn a full athletic scholarship to Western Illinois University. It is through failure that we learn and begin to build our toolbox of skills necessary to take on all obstacles. It's important to take a risk, invest in ourselves, seek out mentors, and build a network with those you wish to model in all facets of business.

My role at ROC is no different. I am still learning and navigating ways to improve as a leader. I plan, direct, and oversee operations activities in the organization and ensure that we are building and creating solutions for our current and future needs. My goal is to always leave things better than what they were upon my arrival, adopting a transformational leadership mindset into my everyday work and forging new leaders. At ROC, we take a team approach in everything we do and, when necessary, adjust where needed. Any time you do something new, it takes time to develop and master; we just make it look easy. Allow yourself time to grow and to develop. In the end, it will be worth all the failures you endured.

MY REAL ESTATE INSPIRATION

Acquiring your real estate license affords you entrepreneurship status and the opportunity to establish your own book of business and to create your own schedule. Your income will depend upon a number of factors, including experience, hours worked, market conditions, and specializations. Like any profession, when you put in the time and effort, the results will not disappoint. Real estate has changed the lives of many of our brokers at ROC, and we openly share our stories of success to inspire others to do the same.

Real estate has long been the honey hole of creating wealth over time. It is how many real estate moguls and developers, like Stephan Alan Wynn, Dottie Herman, Andrew Carnegie, and Donald Trump, have been successful. Money makes more money.

Homeownership generates economic freedom, provides long-term security, and offers unlimited options over other types of investments. Moreover, it is important to ROC because we cater to a Hispanic/Latino clientele that makes up more than half of the nation's population growth and has an upward trajectory in homeownership rates. This data serves our mission to create generational wealth and drives us to serve more families.

BIOGRAPHY

Sally Delgado is the vice president of operations at Realty of Chicago (ROC), a thriving brokerage firm with five locations, award-winning distinctions and recognitions, and a growing roster of over 300 agents. Prior to her appointment, Sally served as an educator with over a decade of experience, ranging from non-profit organizations, post-secondary, and higher education. Sally leads with confidence, a solution-focused mindset, and an unmatched track record of achievements. She is known for her energy and innate ability to connect with people.

Sally is an alumna of DePaul University, where she was recognized for the Latino Student Leadership Award among her peers. She is an alumna of the Hispanic Alliance for Career Enhancement's Mujeres de HACE cohort 2020, an ambassador for St. Jude Children Research Hospital, and served on the Casa Central Auxiliary ELAB board. Sally is looking forward to amplifying the ROC brand and strategic development while bolstering the broker and clientele experience.

Sally Delgado, MED
Sally@realtyofchicago.com
Facebook: @sallydelgado

MY AMERICAN DREAM

GINA DIAZ

"Thanks to my determination and the opportunities in real estate, I made my dream a reality."

Ever since I was a little girl, I would close my eyes and dream of one day taking my whole family to Hawaii. I wanted to feel the warm sun on my face, shining off the palm trees, and the smooth breeze blowing my light auburn locks behind me.

Then I would open my eyes and reality would return. I was in Little Village—a south side neighborhood in Chicago—in my parent's living room that converted into my bedroom at night. I was just a girl from a little village in Guanajuato, Mexico, where having water and electricity was a luxury. I had never been to Hawaii, but I could revisit the dream anytime I closed my eyes.

THE DREAM IS BORN

I spent most of my infancy with my mother in Mexico. My dad went to the United States on his own to search for a job, so he could eventually move our family there. When we eventually crossed the border to reunite with my dad, I only spoke my native language—Spanish. Our new home in Chicago was nothing like my home village in Guanajuato, beginning with English as the spoken language.

In this foreign world, I struggled to learn English, but eventually succeeded. My parents both worked low-paying factory jobs, but they still managed to put me into a private school where I learned to take my education seriously. I saw how hard my mom and dad worked for their wages; and from a young age, I knew education would be my ticket to a comfortable life where we would never be without water or electricity again.

I studied hard and received a scholarship to attend a private high school, which my family could not have otherwise afforded. During the infamous Chicago winters, I'd take a 45-minute bus ride to get to school. I wanted to be an actress and even tried out for the school plays. But when acting didn't work out, I wondered what my next step should be. Nobody in my family had ever even graduated from high school.

Well, God had other plans for me. My life after high school was quickly put on hold when I got pregnant with my daughter at the age of nineteen. I was an only child, but my family was barely getting by with just the three of us. Now, I had to consider my baby. It's terrifying to be pregnant at such a young age and have to raise a kid when you are a kid.

I wanted to return to school, so I attended night classes throughout my pregnancy while working at a law firm during the day. I had my beautiful baby girl and became a mother when I was twenty years old. Being that young and responsible for a human will do one of two things for you—either it makes you or it breaks you.

I wasn't going to let it break me; I wanted it to "make me." I got a job in a law firm as a paralegal assistant and continued to go to school. I was always a very outspoken person when it came to standing up for people and fighting for what I believed in. So, when I was promoted from assistant to a full-blown paralegal, I realized that I had a passion for the law. I decided to become a lawyer.

My mother encouraged me to keep working. I was already making more money than my parents, and already living the American dream, according to her. Then I thought about my situation. My parents had set out to find a better life, so if I was going to achieve the American dream, I had to really go for it. I looked into my baby's eyes and knew I had to do it for her as well. I was going to go to law school—for us. I wanted my baby to have a life filled with endless opportunities. I wanted to show her that if I could do it, she could do it better. I wanted my parents to be proud of me and see me achieve the dream they had dreamt for us.

STUDIES AND SACRIFICE

Without a role model to help me get into law school, I didn't know how I would do it. I only knew I would, and I was up for the challenge. Law school isn't cheap, but it's not impossible. As a first-generation student, I maneuvered through applications and loans all by myself, with a baby depending on me the entire time. It was hard, but I did it.

I was admitted into a law school in Michigan, hours away from my daughter and parents. It was hard when my parents would call and tell me about my daughter's achievements when I was too far away to see. Weekends were never sufficient, but they made my semesters go by faster. All I had to do was make it to the weekend, where I could go back home and see the reason for my dream.

In 2007, I graduated law school in Michigan. My seven-year-old daughter and immigrant parents drove there to see me walk the stage. My heart filled with joy, knowing I was about to embark on the ride of a lifetime.

Once back home, I needed to study for the bar exam, but also needed to help provide for my family. So, I decided to get my real estate license. The people I had met up to that point had mentioned that real estate was an excellent, lucrative career with a lot of flexibility. I was sold. I enrolled in classes and earned my real estate license. During the crash of 2008, I was fortunate enough to close on two deals before I took my bar exam. Then, the market dried up.

I was OK, though. I realized I was a lawyer! I could practice real estate law and help as an agent or as a lawyer because I had both licenses. Woohoo! *Now I will make lots of money*, I thought.

STRUGGLE FOR THE DREAM

When people talk about the American dream, they fail to leave out the amount of first-generation debt that comes along with it. I had a new law degree, but also a seven-year-old who required food, clothes, and shelter. This realization created instant gratitude towards my parents for their help in raising my daughter when I was in Michigan earning my degree. Few people can say their parents gave them that kind of support in their college years. I knew I needed to return the favor.

I began working at a couple of law firms where I gained immense experience. However, I still was not satisfied. Surely this couldn't be it, right? I mean, I had a real estate license, and I was an attorney—when was I going to see all this income everyone expected from me?

In 2010, my husband encouraged me to open my own law firm. I was hesitant and scared, but he assured me that everything would be okay—and that if it wasn't, he'd be there for me. So, I opened my own law firm in Brighton Park, a neighborhood in Chicago, Illinois. Becoming a businesswoman overnight was stressful, to say the least. Suddenly I had to manage cases and meet with clients while figuring out how to set up payroll for my small team. Just like my five-year-old, Spanish-speaking self, I adapted.

Soon my clientele was building, and my business was growing—but not steadily, and I certainly didn't have a financial safety net. Some days I didn't know if my credit card transaction would go through, and my increasing student debt didn't make things easier. I had to keep working and take whatever cases I could to make ends meet.

In 2010 and 2012, I had two more daughters, followed by

an unexpected case of ovarian cancer in 2013. Thank God I was cancer-free after one painful surgery, but let me just say—babies and cancer are very expensive.

For years, I saved up for a deposit to own my own law building. I had rented and leased office space until 2017, when I finally made my first big girl purchase and bought my new law office in Berwyn, Illinois. I thought, *this is it. This is the American dream. I am officially a bad ass. Now, maybe I can save some money and buy another property in five years.*

I accomplished much on my own and even helped my parents become U.S. citizens in 2017 and 2018. However, my finances were a reoccurring struggle.

THE DREAM ACHIEVED

Everyone has this image of a wealthy attorney living the life. The truth is, you graduate with more debt than motivation. Still, I pondered these stereotypes and wondered why I wasn't living a lavish lawyer lifestyle. I struggled to pay my phone bills, while other attorneys spent their spare change on Louis Vuitton bags. When was that going to be me?

In 2018, my friend invited me to the Andrew Holmes' three-day conference. At this point, I was not new to networking events. You meet people, exchange contacts, promise to stay in touch, and then never speak again. I was not going to waste my time. My friend encouraged me, and my husband was sold once he heard it was a real estate seminar. The next thing I knew I was sitting in on a workshop that would change my life.

I had a real estate license and I was an attorney managing her own law firm—I'd like to consider myself an educated woman. However, you don't know what you don't know. By that, I mean you can have endless degrees and endless certificates. Still, until you sit and listen to how you can use those skills in conjunction with one another, you will remain clueless.

My husband and I became a real estate duo, where I handled the legalities and he dealt with the physical work of scouting rentals and fixing them up. I was hesitant to go to that seminar but ended up making some lifelong friendships. I became so passionate about real estate that I felt like the fruits of my labor were paying off. I was combining my passions for real estate and law in a profitable way.

In 2018, I even launched a women's real estate investing group with my best friends. It's called We Win LLC, and it is geared towards teaching other women how to become real estate investors and acquire wealth through real estate.

Since then, my husband and I have acquired more than thirty rental properties, and we don't plan on stopping. It brings me an inexplicable amount of security and comfort to know that my daughters will be OK long after I'm gone and that their daughters will be OK, too.

I fully support my parents, who no longer have to work. I can manage to put my three daughters through college. I feel financially confident for the first time, and I can even treat myself to an occasional Louis Vuitton! Real estate has gifted me moments that I only thought possible in my wildest dreams.

In 2021, I felt the warm sun on my face with the smooth Hawaiian breeze blowing my light auburn locks behind me. I turned to my right and saw my mom, dad, husband, and three children enjoying the Hawaiian breeze along with me. The ability to take my entire family on a trip to Hawaii was something I dreamt of as a little girl. Thanks to my determination and the opportunities in real estate, I made my dream a reality.

MY REAL ESTATE INSPIRATION

I would say it's a career with longevity as there are so many aspects and possibilities with helping people in real estate. Getting a real estate license in addition to practicing real estate law gives you a good idea of all sides of a real estate transaction and opens up the possibilities even further. There's more to real estate than your usual closing. If I would've known that investing in real estate would get me closer to my financial goals, I would've started investing sooner. If you have a passion for real estate and for helping other, you can make a great living in addition to a successful career, however, you must have patience and commitment. Real estate has helped me achieve many personal, financial and professional goals I set to accomplish in my life without even knowing real estate was the way to get there.

"If you take care of real estate for 5 years, real estate will take care of you for the rest of your life."
-Andrew Holmes

BIOGRAPHY

Born in Mexico, Gina Diaz is an accomplished mother of three, ovarian cancer survivor, and attorney who dedicates her time to helping undocumented immigrants in her community. As an immigrant herself, Gina serves her community as one of the top immigration attorneys.

Gina practices within multiple fields of law, including real estate and family law. After being named the top real estate attorney in the state of Illinois, Gina took her knowledge in real estate into the investing field. Gina began building her real estate empire by purchasing and rehabbing properties. After expanding her real estate portfolio with over forty rental properties, she began giving back as one of the founding members of We Win, LLC, an organization dedicated to introducing women to the world of real estate.

Gina decided to make a bigger impact by helping found We Win, NFP, a not-for-profit geared towards transforming lives while providing transitional housing to strengthen communities. Her real estate investments led her to share how to build generational wealth. Gina hopes that people will see themselves in her story and take that first step toward financial security.

Gina Diaz
gina@diazcaselaw.com
Facebook @abogadaginadiaz
Instagram @Diazcase, @Abogadaginadiaz

MAGGIE ANTILLON-MATHEWS

ABOUT THE AUTHOR

Maggie Antillon-Mathews has been in real estate since 2001 and is a multi-million-dollar producer, managing broker, and top agent. She is currently a designated managing broker, trainer, and mentor at Realty of Chicago, where she has served for six years after previously owning her own top-producing company. She is consistently named in the Top 250 in the nation by the National Association of Hispanic Real Estate Professionals® (NAHREP) as well as a Top Producer at Realty of Chicago. She was recently selected as the 2021 Managing Broker of the Year from the Chicago Association of Realtors®.

Maggie also has been featured repeatedly in the Who's Who edition of Chicago Agent Magazine and other local publications, and she co-authored the bestselling book, Latina Empowerment Through Leadership, which was published in 2017 and quickly became a bestseller in Amazon's women's category.

Maggie has helped propel Realty of Chicago from a small real estate company to one of the fastest growing companies in Chicago, and first in the Latino market. Maggie is involved with outreach and community work that is consistent with her values and is committed to sharing her knowledge and experiences with others looking to grow in real estate.

Maggie Antillon-Mathews
maggie@realtyofchicago.com
Facebook: @Maggie.antillonmathews

Made in the USA
Monee, IL
18 November 2023